THE KINGDOM
OF GOD

VOLUME TWO

THE KINGDOM OF GOD

VOLUME TWO

THE SERMON AND THE LIFE

TOM A. JONES
STEVE D. BROWN

www.dpibooks.org

The Kingdom of God—Volume Two
©2011 by DPI Books
5016 Spedale Court #331
Spring Hill, TN 37174

Printed in the United States of America

Cover Design: Brian Branch

ISBN: 978-1-57782-297-4

CONTENTS

Introduction
The Controversial Kingdom

Can the most challenging words we have ever read also be the most encouraging? Can a serious call to live an impossible dream not depress us but transform us? The answer to both questions is "yes" if those words are the message of Jesus that we usually call the Sermon on the Mount found in Matthew 5–7.

In our first volume on the Kingdom of God we pointed out that the Kingdom of God was Jesus' primary message. We described how Jesus announced the in-breaking of God's future into our present age. We diagrammed it like this (see figure 1).

We saw it was his plan for the people of God, empowered by

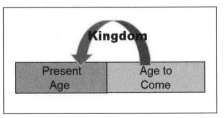

Figure 1

the Holy Spirit, to start living "on earth as it is in heaven." But what does this type of living look like?

Jesus did not leave us guessing. He delivered what we usually call the Sermon on the Mount or what we think could better be called the *Sermon on the Kingdom*.[1] We insisted in Volume One that the Kingdom of God is not just a future to look forward to but a life to be lived here and now. While the Sermon (as we will refer to it most of the time) is not a detailed handbook on every aspect of that life, it is also not a vague statement leaving hearers wondering what they just heard.

In the Sermon are promises about the kind of character God will bless and new commands that are contrasted with their Old Covenant counterparts. In the Sermon we find direction about how to pray and what to be sure of as we pray. Not some announcement of feel-good, self-indulgent religion, the Sermon has stunning words for those who think they are aligned with God but do not really know him. But like Jesus who gave it, the Sermon is full of grace and truth.

Reading the Sermon is not like reading a science book or a tome on the law. What we hear will in large part be determined by the condition of our hearts. Those who read it and are eager to receive the Kingdom will hear a call to a challenging but exciting venture into age-to-come living. Those who want a relationship with God without the kingdom heart will hear annoying restrictions or find themselves shifting immediately to a myriad of "what if" questions and "surely it doesn't mean that" replies.

This is why, through the centuries, the Sermon has been ridiculed by some, treated as a wild ideal or ignored by others, and embraced as a way of life by very few. But that, of course, only underscores the validity of the one who spoke these words, for he said that the way is narrow and few are those who find it.

This much is certain: Jesus' main message was the good news of the Kingdom. After calling people to repent and come to the Kingdom, Matthew's Gospel gives us the Sermon in which he specifically refers to the Kingdom eight times. The very reason the Sermon seems so unreasonable and impractical to some is that it is describing the kingdom life—the life of these "aliens and strangers" from the future. These are the people who are living right now as though they were already in heaven or at least as though they are taking all their direction from heaven, and acting as if their citizenship is really there.

But this much is also certain: Everyone who wants to be a disciple of Jesus must have a most eager heart when coming to the Sermon. Every person who wants to live the kingdom life must see the Sermon as "the Jesus Manifesto" and want his or her life and attitudes toward everything to be shaped by what is either said specifically or the principles revealed.

To be in the Kingdom is to say "Jesus is Lord," and he who is Lord said, "All authority in heaven and on earth is given to me" and then a few phrases later, "teach them to obey everything that I have commanded." If we passionately pursue his words, we will be drawn to the Sermon, for there we find a rather complete package of what he commanded.

Toward the end of the Sermon Jesus compares the way of the Kingdom—the way to life—to a narrow road. As we think of the journey ahead of us, let's consider a few rules for the road.[2]

Rules for the Road

1. *Understand that this is a sermon on the Kingdom.* At the beginning, the Beatitudes are eight crucial statements that form a kind of sandwich starting with a verse that speaks of the Kingdom and ending with a verse that speaks of the Kingdom. What many consider to be the theme statement of the Sermon—"unless your righteousness exceeds the righteousness of the Pharisees and teachers of the law, you will never enter the Kingdom"—obviously has to do with being in the Kingdom. The crucial teaching on prayer in the Sermon calls us to pray for the Kingdom to come. The conclusion of a long section on spiritual living is summed up with the statement "seek first his kingdom and his righteousness." The Sermon ends with Jesus showing how serious he is about living this life when he says, "Not everyone who says to me, 'Lord, Lord,' will enter the kingdom...but only he who does the will of my Father who is in heaven." From beginning to end, this is a Sermon about the Kingdom, which means it is about the coming age breaking now into the present.

2. *Keep in mind that these are the words of Jesus.* You may hear that and think, "I didn't know this book was *The Sermon on the Mount for Dummies.* Who do the writers think they are?" But we point out the obvious because of the tendency we have seen in ourselves, first of all, and then in others to begin to debate these words as if they are open to debate. No, for disciples of Jesus this is his Manifesto— his intentions, his objective, his goals. These are his words, and our role is to say, "Speak, Lord, your servant is listening."

3. *Remember that the Kingdom of God is all about living by the principles of the age to come, which are so contradictory to what the world teaches us.* These are words for those in the Kingdom who now have their citizenship in heaven and take their direction from there. What we will find in the Sermon will be counter-intuitive and a dramatic reversal of the world's values. Don't be surprised if your flesh objects and your mind looks for excuses to go another way.

In my earlier book on Jesus, I (Tom) told of how Philip Yancey writes about a friend who taught at a major university in a part of the country where the Bible is often held in high regard. When she assigned an essay for students to write their reactions to the Sermon on the Mount, she was taken aback by what she read. For the most part, they found it full of unreasonable expectations. Some shared that it made them feel very uncomfortable. One student described it as stupid and inhuman.[3]

The students' candid reactions clearly show that the kingdom lifestyle that Jesus taught is dramatically unlike what most people think of as a healthy way to live. Even those who are more charitable have found it to contain a utopian message that could not be seriously practiced.

4. *Realize there is no way to live this life on our own power.* The more we read these teachings of Jesus, the more we may find ourselves saying, "God have mercy on us." The Sermon starts with a beatitude ("blessed are the poor in spirit") that is a confession that we are spiritual beggars, that we cannot do this without help. But each of the Beatitudes is a reminder of the grace that God intervenes to give his people. Of the "poor in spirit" Jesus says, "theirs is the Kingdom"! They taste the powers of the coming age (Hebrews 6:5). They receive strength to turn and live a new way.

In Matthew's Gospel before the Sermon, we have this statement of Jesus in chapter 4: "From that time on Jesus began to preach, 'Repent, for the Kingdom of heaven has come near'" (v17 Holman). In calling people to repentance (*metanoia*), he was calling for a radical change of mind and heart that would not only involve a commitment to a whole new way of conduct but to a whole new dependence on God for the power to live that new life.

It can be no accident that as Jesus gives these teachings, he includes two vital sections on prayer—one in chapter 6 and one in chapter 7. If we fail to trust in and rely on the "much more of the heavenly Father" (7:11), we will find our engine sputtering on Jesus' narrow road, our wheels stuck in a rut, or the car careening off a ledge. We can agree that the Sermon makes us even more aware of our need for God's grace and mercy, but we must also hear that God will give both.

As Glen Stassen and David Gushee say in their recent book, *Kingdom Ethics: Following Jesus in the Contemporary Context*, what is described in the Beatitudes is "participative grace."[4] In contrast to the "cheap" and one-sided grace Bonhoeffer so famously described, participative grace grasps us, teaches us, trains us and empowers us to live the new life.

Trying to live the Sermon on the kingdom life without the grace of God is like an ordinary person trying to climb Everest without an oxygen tank. Apart from God's grace, the message of this sermon will either wear you out or turn you into a legalist who wears everybody else out. In neither case will you find the Kingdom.

5. *Understand that these injunctions are really to be put into practice. This life is really to be lived.* If there is any one view of the Sermon that has been dominant through the years, it is the view that it is an ideal to inspire and call us higher, but not really a life to be lived.

Stassen and Gushee begin their aforementioned book with an introduction titled "The Problem: The Evasion of Jesus and the Sermon on the Mount."[5] Calling attention to the avoidance of Jesus' teaching they write, "[this] raises the question of exactly who is functioning as Lord of the

Church."[6] An older out-of print work on the Sermon on the Mount by Harvey McArthur began with a chapter titled "Versions and Evasions of the Sermon on the Mount."

In some traditions a serious commitment to the Sermon on the Mount is only for those in certain religious orders, and not to be expected from the ordinary believer. This line of thinking dates to the days of Thomas Aquinas.

In other traditions the Sermon is viewed as teaching that is not to be lived but is simply given to make us conscious of our need for God's grace. This was the strong view of Luther. There is no doubt the Sermon makes us aware of our need for grace and keeps bringing us all back to the first beatitude, which we will shortly explore. But the grace of God that we find there and throughout the Beatitudes "teaches us to say 'No' to ungodliness and worldly passions, and to live self-controlled, upright and godly lives in this present age, while we wait for the blessed hope [in the age to come]" (Titus 2:12–13).

It is surely testimony to man's capacity to avoid the obvious that scholars and common people have ignored Jesus' clear teaching at the end of the Sermon:

> "Therefore everyone who hears these words of mine and puts them into practice is like a wise man who built his house on the rock. The rain came down, the streams rose, and the winds blew and beat against that house; yet it did not fall, because it had its foundation on the rock. But everyone who hears these words of mine and does not put them into practice is like a foolish man who built his house

on sand. The rain came down, the streams rose, and
the winds blew and beat against that house, and it
fell with a great crash." (Matthew 7:24–27)

Jesus could hardly make it plainer. He is not giving us
pious platitudes. He is not painting a dreamy picture of some
unlivable ideal. He is describing the age-to-come lifestyle,
and he is expecting his followers to put it into practice.

We had the disturbing experience of recently asking a
group of ministers to rate the emphasis that had been given
to the Sermon on the Mount in their churches. These men
came from congregations that preach a high level of commitment and call people to be serious disciples of Jesus. On
a scale from 1 to 10, with 10 being high, several of them
said "0." Others thought the average would be about "4."

While these churches had not declared the Sermon on
the Mount to be just an ideal, they had, in effect, sent that
message by neglecting it. Frankly, that is shocking. In our
quest to make disciples, some of us have failed to teach
them what Jesus spells out in Matthew's Gospel before he
gets to anything else.

We will not find another place where such a complete
body of Jesus' teaching is found. It is time we realize that
we must teach disciples to obey everything he taught in this
sermon. This is the kingdom life, and as citizens of heaven
we are to live it.

6. *See the Sermon as describing the way of the cross.*
Though the word "cross," is not found in these three chapters,

its message is everywhere. Every beatitude embodies the idea of losing your life and finding it—that's the way of the cross. Going the second mile is the way of the cross. Not using force to resist the evil person—what else is that but the way of the cross? Not entering the lawsuit world is the way of the cross. Not storing up possessions is the way of the cross.

Not giving into your sexual lust is being crucified with Christ. Loving your enemy is the way of the cross. Saying, your Kingdom come, *your will be done, not mine*—that is the way of the cross.

Nothing is more a reversal of the world's values than the way of the cross. That's why so many people have trouble with the Sermon. The Jews expected the Kingdom of God to come with "shock and awe," with devastating and overwhelming power, blowing the enemies of God away. But Jesus is the suffering servant Isaiah foretold, and the Kingdom is revealed in sacrificial love. In Volume One we included this quote from John Howard Yoder, but we feel it needs to be repeated:

> Here at the cross is the man who loves his enemies, the man whose righteousness is greater than that of the Pharisees, who being rich became poor, who gives his robe to those who took his cloak, who prays for those who despitefully use him. The cross is not a detour or hurdle on the way to the Kingdom, nor is it even the way to the Kingdom; *it is the Kingdom come* (emphasis added).[7]

Jesus was living the cross long before he died on it. And wherever he lived it, the Kingdom was breaking in. He loved his enemies. He prayed for them. He did good to them. He did not strike back. Do you want to know what it looks like to take up your cross and follow Jesus? Read the Sermon on the Mount.

And so here's the rule for the road: If we are ever having trouble with the Sermon and not wanting to obey, we must admit to ourselves that we are having trouble with the cross.

7. *We must realize that our emotions and our traditions can become obstacles to understanding and putting this message into practice.* Over the centuries those calling themselves Christians have developed all kinds of nifty ways to dilute the message that we find here. As many of us have seen when it comes to other biblical issues, traditions are extremely powerful. Only the most earnest and sincere are able to go against the grain of tradition. Equally powerful are our emotions. When the words of Jesus send us one direction but our emotions pull us in another, it is often the emotions that win. At many points in the Sermon we must be ready for a fierce battle. We must be ready to demonstrate ultimate allegiance to God and his Son, for that indeed is what the Kingdom is all about.

8. *The Beatitudes are at the beginning for a reason. They are the key to everything else.* However, we will save our examination of this point for the next chapter.

Ready for a Challenge

So are you ready to go? Just ahead lie challenges such as these:

"Do not lust."

"Do not be angry with your brother."

"Don't resist an evil person."

"Turn the other cheek."

"Love your enemies."

"Be perfect as your father in heaven is perfect."

"Do not let the left hand know what the right hand is doing."

"Pray, your will be done on earth as it is in heaven."

"Don't lay up treasures on earth, but lay up treasures in heaven."

"Do not judge."

"Seek first the kingdom of God."

"Do to others as you would have them do to you."

These are all imperatives from what is still the most radical sermon ever preached. It is a spiritual Mount Everest, rising high above normal ethics, religion and spirituality. To stand at its base and contemplate living its message humbles every heart that sees it clearly. To actually leave the security of the flatlands and climb toward its peak is to embark on a journey that can only be completed by the receiving of abundant grace.

Few are those who will commit themselves to living this life. Preferring a broader way, the "many" will turn away from this narrow path that tests our resolve, determination and spiritual conviction. So taught Jesus at the end of the Sermon.

But this is a book for the "few"—those who will take the greatest challenge, those who will abandon themselves to the will of God though it looks to be an impossible calling. It is for those who are willing to be called a fool, a fanatic or worse because they are confident that no one ever spoke with authority like the one who spoke these words.

You will not need any theological degrees for this journey. You will not need a great intellect. You will not need rare insight. But, as we will see, you will need a humble heart. While we appreciate the value of scholarship, we have not written this book for the scholars. We have written it for the ordinary man, woman, college student and teenager for whom Jesus said the Kingdom is good news. It is for the weak, the crushed, the sinful, the repeat offenders and the simple (or at least for all those who realize that's really who we are).

The Kingdom is about a banquet for the dispossessed that comes because of the "much more of the Heavenly Father" given to those who know they do not deserve it, but celebrate the blessings it brings.

Courage to Accept the Challenge

We write believing that it will take extraordinary courage to live and practice these words. That is why it is so rarely done. But it is time for us to stop making excuses. It is time to stop talking about how hard this is. It is time to say, "Speak, Lord, your servants are listening and ready to follow you."

Yes, it is hard. It is counter-cultural, counter-intuitive and very much at odds with our sinful nature. But Jesus came to set us free from all the things that keep us from living the kingdom life. So, which side of that spectrum are we going to put our emphasis—the "hard" side or the Jesus side? On which side are we going to take our stand?

Right in the Sermon we will find Jesus showing us how we can live this new life and promising us God's resources. His follower Paul said "the kingdom of God is not a matter of talk but of power." It is time for us to believe this. Talking about how hard it is and ending there does nothing but leave us stuck in the ditch on some religious road. "This is the victory that overcomes the world: even our faith," wrote a man who had been following this "hard" way for decades and was still passionate about it.

We are confident that to those who humble themselves before God all things are possible and that he will give the courage so his people can be a light in the darkness and a city set on a hill.

Shall we have another intellectual exercise on the Sermon on the Mount and talk it to death and come away with no conviction, ending up with a quaint but irrelevant document from religious history? God forbid! The need of the hour is for people who will call Jesus "Lord, Lord," and then cry out, "And we *will* do what you say!"

A spine-tingling, rip-roaring, downright dangerous adventure awaits us. And on top of this, it is one that really matters. The writer of Hebrews describes Jesus as the *archagos* of our faith. Various translations have "author," "champion," "founder" and at least one says "pioneer." And that may be getting close to what the writer intended. The word can also be translated "trailblazer," and that is who Jesus is. He is blazing a trail to a brave new world. Sure, uncharted territory can be scary, but we don't follow because it seems so safe or because it makes so much sense to us. We follow because we trust him who goes before us, and as he did, we entrust ourselves to him who judges justly.

Context of Making Disciples

One more thing we need to remember as we look at this teaching as recorded in verse two of chapter 5 in Matthew's Gospel. This sermon is delivered in the context of discipleship training. Jesus was not primarily a public speaker. The model he set for us was not to deliver grand discourses. Over and over the New Testament calls our attention to his focus on "his disciples," and when it was time to wrap it all up and return to the Father, his last words were left with them. His first mountain speech is the focus of this book, but we must not study it without a consciousness of his last mountain speech recorded in Matthew 28:18–20:

> Then Jesus came to them and said, "All authority in heaven and on earth has been given to me. Therefore go and make disciples of all nations, baptizing

> them in the name of the Father and of the Son and
> of the Holy Spirit, and teaching them to obey every-
> thing I have commanded you. And surely I am with
> you always, to the very end of the age."

If we divorce the Sermon on the Kingdom from the everyday business of making disciples, then it becomes a mere homily on ethics or a theoretical discourse on morals. At the heart of what Jesus did was to work with the few that committed themselves to follow him and shape them into the men they were meant to be. The Sermon has to be taken in this context—the making of disciples. Those who take the sermon seriously will be busy making disciples.

Jesus is calling us to follow in his steps—just like his disciples did 2000 years ago.

Questions for Study and Discussion

1. What is your understanding of what Jesus meant by "the Kingdom of God," and how does it relate to the Sermon on the Mount?
2. What feelings or attitudes have you had toward the Sermon in the past?
3. Of the "Rules for the Road" described here, which ones do you believe you must pay particular attention to?
4. Are there any fears you have about wholeheartedly committing yourself to live the Sermon?
5. What promises from God will you have to rely on to live this message?
6. Do you want to obey everything Jesus teaches in this sermon?

1
Kingdom Attitudes

When we think of the relationship of the Beatitudes to the rest of the Sermon, numerous analogies and metaphors come to mind.

If we envision the life this sermon describes as a great spiritual mountain that we wish to climb, the Beatitudes should be seen as the boots that every climber will tell you are so essential. Without a grasp of the Beatitudes, our journey through the rest of chapter 5, into chapter 6 and on through chapter 7 will be quite miserable. We will have some pretty severe blisters before we ever get to something like "don't resist an evil person."

To change the image, the Beatitudes are like the alphabet; you must learn them early, but you will be using them for the rest of the way. Try to skip them, and your spiritual life will end up being only so much gibberish.

In a similar way, trying to live this sermon on the Kingdom without internalizing the Beatitudes, would be like trying to play basketball before you ever master the art of dribbling and passing. And just as a coach will often bring his team back to focus on these basics when their play becomes ragged and sloppy, so we must be brought back to these crucial attitudes again and again as we seek to live this kingdom life.

This is what enables us to see the Sermon as something other than a hopeless ideal. It is staying grounded in the Beatitudes that creates the spiritual dynamic to keep living this high call.

It is interesting that we call these the Beatitudes, for they are the essential kingdom attitudes that need to *be* in all our lives. (That works fine in English, but, of course, not at all when it is translated into other languages.)

When we find Jesus' words in this sermon irritating us, frustrating us or burdening us, a key rule for the road is go back to the Beatitudes. When our relationships with fellow travelers are broken or not close, go back to the Beatitudes. Our convictions about these eight qualities are so strong that we will devote a disproportionate amount of space to considering them.

Import of the Beatitudes

Most translations of Matthew 5:1–2 read similar to the NIV: "Now when he went up on a mountainside and sat down, his disciples came to him, and he began to teach them, saying..." Young's Literal Translation, which often reads awkwardly, attempts to capture what is difficult to translate into English: "and having opened his mouth, he was teaching them, saying...." The verb tense is the imperfect, which in Greek describes continuous or repeated action in past time. So the idea is that this is the teaching Jesus habitually offered.

Therefore, we tend to think that because of the import of the Beatitudes, Jesus must have shared similar thoughts on more occasions than the two recorded in Matthew and Luke (6:20–26).When Luke tells us in Acts that during the forty days after his resurrection he was teaching the disciples about the Kingdom of God (Acts 1:3), it wouldn't surprise us if he were still reminding them of the Beatitudes.

It is our observation that just about everything we are called to do in the rest of the Sermon, or in the rest of the New Testament for that matter, can be traced in some way back to the Beatitudes. Because of this, we will benefit greatly by focusing carefully on them.

A New Heart

In the remainder of the Sermon, Jesus will share specifics that to some listeners may have sounded like new laws given to replace old ones. But this understanding would have missed the point. Jesus is bringing a whole new emphasis on the heart, not instituting a new law. The Beatitudes then are about the new heart we have on the inside after hearing the call to the Kingdom and repenting (Matthew

4:17). This teaching is reiterated in Matthew 23:26, where Jesus admonishes the Pharisees to "first clean the inside of the cup and dish, and then the outside also will be clean." Right actions will follow right hearts.

Blessed Are...

Each of these statements begins "Blessed are...." The Greek word that is translated "blessed" is the word *markarios*. There is no English word that translates it perfectly. In some of the more modern versions it is rendered as "happy," which does not do justice to the deeper meaning of joy and wholeness unaffected by outward circumstances.

It may be that the word *markarios* did not itself fully do justice to the word that Jesus most likely used in speaking this message in Aramaic. This word he most likely used is *ashrei*, and in Judaism it carried with it not only the idea of a blessing but the idea of a calling, specifically a call to action. So while the Greek word *markarios* ("blessed") sounds somewhat passive, the Aramaic word is active. Part of its meaning was even the idea of "wake up" or "get up" or "stand up" or "arise."

That Jesus meant it this way is a fascinating possibility because instead of the passive "Blessed are the poor in spirit" you would have something more like "Stand up, you poor in spirit" or "Arise, you who are meek." We have already referred to Stassen and Gushee's idea that the Beatitudes describe "participative grace." This certainly fits with these possibilities from the Aramaic. The Beatitudes describe grace that we receive but also grace that calls us into action.

But let us make three more observations about the Beatitudes.

1. These attitudes are for every Christian.

In the history of Christendom, various groups have suggested that these qualities will be found only in certain extra-spiritual people, but this is a distortion of the truth. The same could be said of thinking that one of these may be "my strength." *All* these attitudes are for *all* disciples.

2. The Beatitudes most likely are a progression.

They fit together, and it even appears that each one leads to the next. This insight we first gained from D.M. Lloyd-Jones fits with so much that is in Scripture and proves invaluable in understanding the "spiritual formation" that Jesus is bringing to our lives. We are surprised at how many writers, even some of our favorites, pull the Beatitudes apart and look at them as free-standing ideas. This does not fit with the key idea in biblical interpretation—to consider first the context, nor does it give Jesus credit for choosing to order his words as he does.

3. The Beatitudes will often greatly clash with the 'world's wisdom.'

This is because they represent the heart found in those who live by the age to come. The world seldom applauds the poor in spirit, but rather lifts up the self-confident. It wants to laugh not mourn...and meekness? The world says, "Who needs that?" You can list the eight kingdom attitudes on one side of a piece of paper and easily come up with eight qualities on the other side that are contradictory and yet exalted by the world. Friedrich Nietzsche saw these verses embodying a slave morality typical of Christians, and James Joyce, William Blake and others condemned them for advocating a life without striving. We can be sure of this: These are not simply nice platitudes. They represent a radical change of heart—one very offensive and even threatening to the spirit of this world. There is a reason the last beatitude is about how kingdom people will be persecuted.

The Beatitudes are the heart and soul of kingdom thinking. They are counter-cultural in nature because they reject the dominant values and behavior of society. They are also counter-intuitive, going against the very grain of what one would normally expect. They are opposed in every way to what the world calls "conventional wisdom."

So with these thoughts in mind, we are ready to put on our hiking boots, study our ABCs and understand kingdom transformation that works from the inside out.

Questions for Study and Discussion

1. Was there any new thought for you in this chapter? How did it have impact on you?
2. How do you see the Beatitudes clashing with "the world's wisdom" as it may show up in your life?
3. For Nietzsche to say the Beatitudes describe a "slave mentality" shows that he was missing what truths about the Kingdom of God?
4. Why will it be so crucial to get the Beatitudes and come back to them again and again in order to live the kingdom life?
5. Do you want to have every one of these kingdom attitudes in your life?

2
The Poor in Spirit

"Blessed are the poor in spirit,
for theirs is the kingdom of heaven."

Matthew 5:3

We should not be surprised to find that the first beatitude spoken by Jesus is the key to being in the Kingdom and living everything Jesus taught. "Blessed are the poor in spirit, for theirs is the kingdom of heaven." With this statement Jesus makes it clear, without using the word, that his message is going to be based on grace. The most common way of reading the Sermon is to see it representing a performance model. But the first beatitude makes it clear that it is a grace model.

Who will be in the Kingdom? It will not be those who hold up their shiny spiritual trophies or take pride in their accomplishments. No, it will be those who acknowledge their poverty of spirit. There were two words in Greek that could mean poor. One, *penés,* meant so poor that you did not own property. The other, *ptóchos*, meant poor to the point that you had to beg. *Ptóchos* had its roots in the idea of being bent over or cowering. It had to do with desperation and destitution. It is this second word that appears here.

So, amazingly, it would appear that Jesus is saying those who will be blessed by God with entrance into the Kingdom will be those who realize and acknowledge that they are spiritual beggars. The beginning point, the A in the ABCs, is not an assertion that "I am going to be strong and courageous and committed," but it is a confession that "I am in great need."

Jesus would later call for people to count the cost before deciding to follow him. But the kingdom life does not begin with a statement that says, "I have counted the cost and I can do it." The life of a disciple begins with an admission that I am poor—that I need help—that I come as a spiritual beggar. Maybe one of the best illustrations of this beatitude is found in Luke 18:9–14:

> To some who were confident of their own right-eousness and looked down on everybody else, Jesus told this parable:
>
> "Two men went up to the temple to pray, one a Pharisee and the other a tax collector. The Pharisee stood up and prayed about himself: 'God, I thank you that I am not like other men—robbers, evildoers, adulterers—or even like this tax collector. I fast twice a week and give a tenth of all I get.'
>
> "But the tax collector stood at a distance. He

would not even look up to heaven, but beat his breast and said, 'God, have mercy on me, a sinner.'

"I tell you that this man, rather than the other, went home justified before God. For everyone who exalts himself will be humbled, and he who humbles himself will be exalted."

Polar Opposites

If there is someone who is poor in spirit, then there would also be his opposite who would be "rich" in spirit. This instructive story provides examples of both. One man far exceeds the other in religiosity and impressive spiritual accomplishments. But his own achievements form the basis of his security. We know that he thinks about righteousness, but his problem is that he is confident of his own righteousness. Most likely he is like the people that Jesus would describe later in the Sermon—he prayed, fasted (in his case, twice a week), and gave alms. Religion was his life, but his idol was himself. From high up on top of his achievements, he looked down on everybody else. He thanked God that he was not like other men, especially this tax collector.

The other man was his polar opposite. The tax collector was a member of a despised group in Jesus' day. Remember, Jesus is telling a parable; he could have given this man any profession, but he picked one everyone despised.

The Pharisees would not have been the only ones to look down on tax collectors. Most everyone would have. But as Jesus describes him, the tax collector is not looking down on anyone. He's not comparing himself to others and saying, "At least I don't do that." Broken in spirit over his sin, he would not even look up to heaven. But he was very much focused on God, crying out for his mercy.

Then Jesus says something that echoes throughout the New Testament: "I tell you that this man, rather than the other, went home justified before God." We wish people today could understand how startling that would've been to Jesus' first-century hearers. The Pharisee was the religious scholar and practitioner. He undoubtedly knew far more "Bible" than the tax collector. But the tax collector saw something the scholar did not see. He saw how desperately he needed God and God's grace.

Jesus says it clearly: The tax collector "went home justified [right] before God." To use words Paul would use later in Romans, he was given the righteousness of God. Righteousness was credited to his account.

On the other hand, the very religious man did not go home justified. He did not go home with God. He went home with himself and his self-righteousness, which in reality was filthy rags.

Confidence in God's Faithfulness

We should notice to whom Jesus spoke this parable. It was "to some who were confident of their own righteousness and looked down on everybody else." When we are poor in spirit, there are two things we do not do: We do not put our confidence in our own righteousness, and we do not look down on others. It is difficult to see when we are doing the first, but it is fairly easy to see when we are doing the second. When we see this attitude in ourselves, it should humble us, bring us to our knees and find us saying, "God, be merciful to me, a sinner."

Those who are poor in spirit can have great confidence, but it will come from God's faithfulness, not from their own performance. Like the proverbial beggar who has found bread, we will want to pass on to others what we have learned. That will certainly involve teaching others and sometimes even correcting others, but it will never involve looking down on them.

It is rather amazing how the rest of the Sermon has a way of driving us back to this first beatitude again and again. The high calling in the rest of the message will humble us and bring us back to confess our poverty of spirit. This is not a bad thing because over and over it will bring us to a fresh appreciation of the Kingdom. Just as the Parable of the Tax Collector and the Pharisee is a great affirmation of how God's grace comes to us, so this first beatitude—the opening statement of this great sermon, the foundation on which everything else will be built—is a powerful affirmation that the kingdom life begins by grace and continues by grace.

Jesus will go on later in the Gospels to describe the Kingdom as treasure in a field, as a pearl of great value, as a great banquet; and who is it that will be given this great gift of the Kingdom? It will be those who continue to humbly acknowledge their great need for God and his mercy.

We learn in John 3 that it takes a new birth of water and the Spirit to enter the Kingdom of God, but this beatitude helps us to understand that this new birth does not come just from some outward action. It comes when there is an inner conviction of our deep need for God.

Questions About the Beatitudes

Over the past few years, there are some questions we have been asked about this beatitude. We want to share them with you.

1. Is it possible to be too poor in spirit?

The question seems to be motivated by a fear that this beatitude might lead us to some psychologically and spiritually unhealthy places. This question is often raised by someone influenced by the modern view that it is healthy to believe in yourself or by those who have been greatly troubled with what we call a low self-esteem (we will deal with the latter issue shortly).

In trying to answer this, perhaps we should ask, "Can we be too merciful or too pure in heart or too hungry for righteousness?" It is our conviction that one cannot be too poor in spirit if (a) we understand what it really means and (b) we understand how God blesses those who are this way. This beatitude really frees us. It lets us know that we don't have to be in denial about our flaws and weaknesses, but at the same time we don't have to be paralyzed by fear and inadequacy. God has accepted us and God will work in us.

Perhaps it is helpful to look at some great biblical examples of poverty of spirit. First, there is Isaiah in chapter 6 when he sees the greatness of God and cries out, "I am a man of unclean lips and I live among a people of unclean lips." But then he sees God accept that humility and come to him, and he ends up saying, "Here am I, send me." His recognition of his need for God led him to be a man of action.

Then look at Paul. No one did more to spread the message of Jesus in the first century than Paul. But look at his life. At first he was a card-carrying Pharisee. He was a confident, self-righteous man, but after a dramatic, earth-shaking confrontation with Jesus and three days to flounder in his blindness, he faced his sin and admitted his tremendous need for God. Then God picked him up and used him powerfully. And God just kept using him powerfully because throughout his life Paul kept admitting that apart from Jesus, he was in great need. He stayed in poverty of spirit, but was hardly hampered by low self-esteem.

It is instructive to look at three statements in his letters in chronological order and see that Paul kept taking the idea of poverty of spirit even deeper.

First, see what he says in 1 Corinthians 15:9:

> For I am the least of the apostles and do not even deserve to be called an apostle, because I persecuted the church of God.

Some years later writing from prison, he says in Ephesians 3:7–8:

> I became a servant of this gospel by the gift of God's grace given me through the working of his power. Although I am less than the least of all God's people, this grace was given me: to preach to the Gentiles the unsearchable riches of Christ.

Then, finally, near the end of his life, he wrote these words in 1 Timothy 1:15–16:

> Here is a trustworthy saying that deserves full acceptance: Christ Jesus came into the world to save sinners—of whom I am the worst. But for that very reason I was shown mercy so that in me, the worst of sinners, Christ Jesus might display his unlimited patience as an example for those who would believe on him and receive eternal life.

Most likely some advocates of pop psychology would say that Paul was too poor in spirit, but that is not the biblical assessment. He just kept the reality of his need and the reality of God's grace and mercy clearly in mind, and God kept using him. He lost his life and he found it. He lost his self-reliance and self-righteousness and religious pride, but he found God's grace and God's Kingdom.

2. What is the difference between low-self esteem and poverty of spirit?

This answer is oversimplified, but in our experience, low self-esteem is characterized by a focus on self, not on God. The person with low self-esteem is often comparing himself or herself to others and often ends up with the view that

"I'm so bad that God can't use me." There is no faith in low self-esteem.

On the other hand, the person who is poor in Spirit has his or her focus on God. "Yes, I am weak. Yes, I am flawed. Yes, I am a sinner, but when I come to God in humility admitting my need, he embraces me, and that changes everything. Now I can say: 'Here am I, send me.'"

3. What is the best way for us to encourage poverty of spirit?

We are sure that a variety of answers could be given, but it seems to us that an excellent place to start is with 1 John 1:7–10:

> But if we walk in the light, as he is in the light, we have fellowship with one another, and the blood of Jesus, his Son, purifies us from all sin.
> If we claim to be without sin, we deceive ourselves and the truth is not in us. If we confess our sins, he is faithful and just and will forgive us our sins and purify us from all unrighteousness. If we claim we have not sinned, we make him out to be a liar and his word has no place in our lives.

Mark the number of times in this passage that the words "we," "us" and "our" appear along with the idea of fellowship with one another. Isn't it true that staying poor in spirit is a matter of walking in the light with each other, which seems to be parallel to confessing our sins to each other? We have often heard our friend and fellow teacher Gordon

Ferguson say, "I don't confess my sins because I'm so humble. I confess my sins in order that I might stay humble." Openness about what is going on in our lives and even in our minds is surely one of the best ways to maintain poverty of spirit.

So based on the meaning of the Aramaic *ashrei* that we discussed in our introduction to the Beatitudes in chapter 1, Jesus may very well be saying, "Arise, you poor in spirit, and by the grace of God, enjoy the fact that the Kingdom is yours."

Questions for Study and Discussion

1. How does this first beatitude make it clear that the kingdom life is based on a grace model and not a performance model? Why is this so important to keep in mind as we engage the Sermon?
2. What kind of attitudes would you expect to find in the person who is poor in spirit?
3. When we look down on others, what are usually the reasons, and what does this reveal about our hearts?
4. Why is poverty of spirit not just a beginning place but an attitude we must continue with?
5. How do we encourage poverty of spirit in each other's lives?
6. How do others see poverty of spirit in your life?

3
Those Who Mourn

"Blessed are those who mourn,
    for they will be comforted."

Matthew 5:4

On any given day in the cities around the world people
are in mourning over something: loss of physical possessions through fire, storm or accident; missed opportunities; loss of health; or loss of loved ones.

By definition, mourning is not pleasant. It can range from
sadness to deep anguish. Mourning is not a state anyone
looks forward to; it is something we hope to get out of soon.
However, this beatitude makes it clear that the process of
mourning plays a key role in shaping us into kingdom people. But does Jesus have a specific type of mourning in mind?

At first reading this beatitude may sound quite strange—
particularly in a few English translations that say "Happy are
those who mourn" or "Happy are the sad."

We have said already that the Beatitudes contain a totally new look at living, and this beatitude definitely shows us how different God's wisdom is from the world's. But we have also learned that we should not pull these beatitudes out of context. If we keep this verse in context, we realize that this is not some general promise that everyone who mourns is going to end up being blessed and happy. Our experience tells us this just isn't so. Many people who go through mourning for various reasons don't feel that it has brought them to a better place.

So what is Jesus describing? We believe this is one of those times it is helpful to see the Beatitudes as a progression. And it is our opinion that this second beatitude can only be well understood in the context of the first.

In the first beatitude we look at our lives and see our poverty of spirit. We see our sin and our need for God's deliverance. Now in this second beatitude it seems Jesus is taking us deeper and saying, "Blessed is the person who looks at his sin and takes it seriously and mourns over it."

It is often observed that the letter of James contains more allusions to the Sermon on the Mount than any other book in the New Testament. And in chapter 4 James would seem to be echoing what is said in the second beatitude: "Grieve, mourn and wail. Change your laughter to mourning and your joy to gloom." In other words, take your sin seriously.

Author John Stott in his book on the Sermon on the Mount (*Christian Counter Culture*) says this beatitude helps us see the difference between *confession* and *contrition*.[1]

Sometimes there is confession on our part, but no contrition. We intellectually recognize our sin and perhaps even verbally describe it, but we fail to feel deeply sorry for the pain we have brought to God and to others. In context, this beatitude would be calling us to see the consequences of our sin and to go through a time of getting in touch and feeling remorse.

A Solution for Sin

We believe the first two beatitudes need to be looked at as a unit. Doing so would present a strong doctrine of sin—just like that which we find in the rest of the Bible. The Bible's view of sin is that it is lethal—it is destructive. Our sin, first of all, inflicts great pain on God. Consider these words written by Isaiah:

> "You have not bought any fragrant calamus for me,
>   or lavished on me the fat of your sacrifices.
> But you have burdened me with your sins
>   and wearied me with your offenses."
> (Isaiah 43:24)

But sin also affects our families, friends and other people. In the church it damages our relationships. It destroys our ability to reach out to others.

If we think our sins are simply secret transgressions which do not hurt others, we need to understand this is never true. When sin damages us, we are limited in what we are able to be in others' lives. So sin is never something to treat lightly and to sweep under the rug. The world's wisdom tells us to laugh it off. God's wisdom calls us to deal with it honestly.

In the gospel there is good news that brings a solution for sin. Christians are set free, not having to live under a weight of guilt from sin. But to get to God's solution for sin we must be willing to go through "mourning." We must be willing to see sin in all its ugliness.

To bring this concept down to earth and out of the theological clouds, consider some examples of times when we need to face our sin:

- When we first consider making a decision to follow Jesus and look back over the life we have lived.
- When we have been bitter and unforgiving with a brother or sister.
- When we have been erratic, half-hearted in our relationships with others.
- When we as husbands have not provided the kind of spiritual leadership God calls us to in our families.
- When those of you who are wives have not been submissive to and supportive of your husbands.
- When we as children have been selfish and rebellious in our relationship with our parents.

Peace, Peace?

Certainly, this list could be much longer, but we get the idea and we realize the effects of our sin in the lives of others.

Hopefully we do not do what God through the prophet Jeremiah says.

> "From the least to the greatest,
>   all are greedy for gain;
> prophets and priests alike,
>   all practice deceit.
> They dress the wound of my people
>   as though it were not serious.
> 'Peace, peace,' they say,
>   when there is no peace.
> Are they ashamed of their loathsome conduct?
>   No, they have no shame at all;
>   they do not even know how to blush.
> So they will fall among the fallen;
>   they will be brought down when I punish
>   them,"
>   says the LORD. (Jeremiah 6:13–15)

The New American Standard Bible translates verse 14: "And they have healed the brokenness of My people superficially." If we deal with the wounds caused by sin *superficially,* they do not get healed. God's comfort and God's resolution only comes when we do not take sin lightly. There is no guarantee that we will not return to a sin. But when we have faced it honestly and have mourned over it deeply, surely there is much less chance that we will go back to it.

Of course, we cannot talk about this beatitude without referring to Paul's words in 2 Corinthians 7:5–11.

> For when we came into Macedonia, this body of ours had no rest, but we were harassed at every turn—conflicts on the outside, fears within. But God, who comforts the downcast, comforted us by the coming of Titus, and not only by his coming but also by the comfort you had given him. He told us about your longing for me, your deep sorrow, your ardent concern for me, so that my joy was greater than ever.
>
> Even if I caused you sorrow by my letter, I do not regret it. Though I did regret it—I see that my letter hurt you, but only for a little while—yet now I am happy, not because you were made sorry, but because your sorrow led you to repentance. For you became sorrowful as God intended and so were not harmed in any way by us. Godly sorrow brings repentance that leads to salvation and leaves no regret, but worldly sorrow brings death. See what this godly sorrow has produced in you: what earnestness, what eagerness to clear yourselves, what indignation, what alarm, what longing, what concern, what readiness to see justice done. At every point you have proved yourselves to be innocent in this matter.

This passage clearly shows there will be an ongoing need for the second beatitude in the life of the church. There were things not right in the lives of the Corinthian disciples. When Paul wrote his earlier letter, he did not say, "'Peace, peace' when there was no peace." He did not heal the wound superficially. His letter pointed out their sin, and he did it in a way that hurt them and caused them sorrow.

But now he can say, "I am happy, not because you were made sorry, but because your sorrow led you to repentance.

For you became sorrowful as God intended and so were not harmed in any way by us" (emphasis added). Kingdom people must understand that there is a time to mourn and that God intends it, as always, for our good.

In verse 10 Paul makes it clear why this is so important: "Godly sorrow brings repentance that leads to salvation and leaves no regret, but worldly sorrow brings death." Dealing with sin superficially and taking sin lightly will not bring repentance. In such cases, we just aren't allowing ourselves to see it and feel it enough to do anything about it. But godly sorrow (like that described in the second beatitude) brings us to a point of seeking a radical change. And all of this leads to salvation.

> The sacrifices of God are a broken spirit;
> > a broken and contrite heart,
> > O God, you will not despise. (Psalm 51:17)

The promise of the second beatitude is that those who mourn in a godly way will be comforted. We simply must not be afraid to deal seriously with our sin. We must not be protective and convince ourselves not to feel too bad as we give in to the humanistic voices around us. We must realize that when we fully face sin and have godly sorrow for it, we will be comforted.

Parable of the Prodigal Son

If the first beatitude was illustrated by the Parable of the Tax Collector and the Pharisee, then the second beatitude is illustrated by the Parable of the Prodigal Son (Luke 15:18–24). Here we see the son taking his sin seriously, saying, "Father, I have sinned against heaven and against you. I am no longer worthy to be called your son." And then we have the father's response, which speaks to us God's amazing grace and comfort that he gives when we have been broken and contrite.

Neither of us has ever regretted the times we have taken sin seriously in our lives and have come to God in humble repentance. Nor have we known of anyone else who has regretted the same. Think about it. Have you ever known anyone who mourned over their sins this way and were sorry that they had done so?

The word "mourning" is not going to be on anyone's list of favorite words; however this is not a gloomy beatitude. It just tells us that there is no shortcut to God's comfort and God's grace and God's embrace. We can't take a detour around our sin. We can't get to the comfort and love of God through rationalizing or diminishing the effects of sin. We get to the comfort of God by being honest about how ugly it is and sorrowful about the effects of it.

Lose Your Life and Find It

As is true of most of the Beatitudes, this is another example of "lose your life and find it." Facing sin feels like "losing your life" (and surely there is some dying in it), but it leads to finding your life—finding God's forgiveness and the refreshment of God's Spirit. No one can read the New

Testament and think that it is God's plan for his people to live their lives steeped in guilt. The goal of the gospel is for God to be with us, to forgive us, to comfort us, to treat us as his special sons and daughters, and to allow us to participate in his generous grace. "Blessed are those who mourn, for they will be comforted."

Questions for Study and Discussion

1. How do the first and second beatitudes connect and relate to each other?
2. Why do you think we often fail to call each other to practice this beatitude?
3. Why is it important not to try to avoid "mourning" or fail to call others to it?
4. How does this beatitude fit with the truth of the gospel and offer such good news?
5. How does this beatitude affect the way you deal with your sin?

4
The Meek

"Blessed are the meek,
  for they will inherit the earth."

Matthew 5:5

Now we come to arguably the most difficult of the Beatitudes, the one that the world has the most trouble with, and the one that provokes the most ridicule. Bumper stickers are a portal into the way people think. When it comes to being meek, they are not very positive or charitable. Here are a few examples:

> *The meek shall inherit the earth, but the lawyers will take 40%.*
> *If the meek will inherit the earth, what about us tigers!*
> *The meek shall inherit s***.*
> *The meek shall inherit the earth...after the Republicans trash it.*

And the scariest one of all:
The meek shall inherit a violent death.

Consulting a dictionary doesn't clarify the biblical meaning. The definition given by Dictionary.com is: (1) humbly patient or docile, as under provocation from others and (2) overly submissive or compliant; spiritless; tame.

These are not the kind of qualities that people get fired up about or aspire to have in their lives. "Meek" is not a word that you would find in the biographies of the "rich and famous." The truth is that more often than not calling someone meek is intended as an insult.

Strength Under Control

The problem starts with the real difficulty in translating the Greek word *praus.* Although most modern translations still use the word "meek," the NASV translates it "gentle" and the NLT translates it "humble." The Greek word refers to the concept of "strength under control." For example, it is used in reference to a powerful trained stallion after he is broken and is being guided by his rider. Before being trained the horse was powerful and yet its energy was not harnessed or focused, but once the horse has been trained, its energy and power are able to be fully utilized.

We have to keep in mind that we are dealing with a concept foreign to the world we live in, yet found throughout the Bible. In the Old Testament, the meek are those wholly relying on God rather than on their own strength to defend against injustice. We have the example of Moses in Numbers 12:3: "Now the man Moses was very meek, more than all people who were on the face of the earth" (ESV). Remember this is the same person talked about in Psalm 106:23.

> So he said he would destroy them—
>   had not Moses, his chosen one,
> stood in the breach before him
>   to keep his wrath from destroying them.

This is mind-boggling. Here is a human being reasoning with the Almighty God, standing up for what he truly believed was right. So this little four-letter word "meek" is loaded with meaning. It is the opposite of self-assertiveness and self-interest. To be meek is to be fully surrendered to God, which puts one in a position of strength. So, contrary to popular opinion, "meek" does not mean "weak."

The absolute bottom line is this: To be meek is to be like Jesus. For he himself said, "Take my yoke upon you and learn from me, for I am gentle (meek) and humble in heart, and you will find rest for your souls" (Matthew 11:29). This is the Jesus that told a storm to be quiet, who ignored the threats of a king, and who stood the religious world on its head.

We could wish for a better word, but there just doesn't seem to be one in the English language that truly captures the concept of being surrendered and humble, relying on God, and being open and teachable. It basically means to be like Jesus.

Complete Dependence on God

So how does this all fit with the concept that the Beatitudes are a series of steps that we take in our spiritual journey and that they fit together one after another in a logical way? We see our total need for God in the first beatitude, and we confess our sinfulness and inability to do anything about it in the second. In the third beatitude we acknowledge our complete dependence on God and our desperate need to learn to trust him in every situation.

In the context of the kingdom message, meekness has one principle meaning. It means that we come to God, putting our lives under his control and surrendering our agenda. For a first-century Jew like Peter or Simon the Zealot it would mean surrendering the agenda of driving out the Romans and establishing Jewish autonomy. It would mean accepting a new agenda for the Gentiles and pagans. For us as for them being meek means giving up all our agendas—be they social, political or religious—and seeking to bring all our thinking under the reign of God.

Viewing meekness in terms of our relationship with God is one thing, but applying it to our relationships with others takes our Christianity to a whole other level. We cannot be meek in our relationship with God without being surrendered to what he is trying to teach us through others. In other words, humility toward God must be accompanied by humility toward others. In this beatitude we come to the critical quality needed to grow, to be mentored, to be discipled. Pride is the antithesis of each of the first three beatitudes.

The pride that causes us to resist the help of other people has nothing in common with this third beatitude.

Sometimes, there is a tendency to try to change our character in a humanistic manner and thus to become weak and spineless and have no impact on the world around us. Should we have this tendency, looking at Jesus is the best way to find balance. He demonstrates for us what meekness looks like as we relate to our Father and to others.

Trusting God

Let me (Steve) talk personally for a moment. The challenge I face, once I get beyond my negative conceptions of the word, is "Do I really want to be meek?" In the context of the Beatitudes it is clear to me that just as I am called to be poor in spirit and just as I need to mourn, I also have to be meek—that is, if I really want God to work in my life. I have to surrender my life and my will to God. I have to be totally open to God's way of doing things.

I don't think I need to tell you how hard that is. Everything in me wants to hold on to what I want, to who I am. That is the problem. I can never become all that God created me to be unless I surrender completely to him. As Jesus said in other places, it all begins with denying myself, giving up myself, and going the way of the cross.

Our recent move to Texas brought this home again. I was very happy living in Nashville working with the brothers in the ministry there and felt like God really had us there for a purpose. Tom and I were working together teaching and writing about the Kingdom. I was involved as a liaison between the mid-South churches and the Andean group that the Nashville Church supports in South America. We had family there. Both of our widowed moms lived within driving distance. Moving just did not seem to me to make any sense.

God had a different idea. He made it clear. So I had to pray. I had to open up to others and get input so I could get my heart where it needed to be. So here we are in McAllen, Texas. God worked it all out and brought us into a great situation where hopefully we will be able to serve even more effectively.

Inherit the Earth?

The promise that is connected with this beatitude is that the meek will inherit the earth. What does that mean? Well, in one sense it means that they already have. We have inherited the earth. As Paul explains in 2 Corinthians 6:9–10, we already have it all:

> ...known, yet regarded as unknown; dying, and yet we live on; beaten, and yet not killed; sorrowful, yet always rejoicing; poor, yet making many rich; having nothing, and yet possessing everything.

As disciples of Jesus, we possess everything. Our Father owns it all and so it is ours.

Of course, there is another sense, a future sense. As we explained at some length in our first book, there is a sense in which the Kingdom of God is "not yet." Yes, the future has broken in; the Kingdom is here and now, and yet all is not over and done. We have inherited the earth, and yet we are still waiting to do so in the new heaven and the new earth. We have the victory in one sense, but in another sense we are still waiting to be crowned, waiting to inherit all that our Father has for us.

Questions for Study and Discussion

1. How have you thought about meekness in the past, and has it been a quality you desired?
2. Describe what the biblical concept of meekness is and how it would fit with living a kingdom lifestyle.
3. How does being meek before God relate to being meek in our relationships with others?
4. Specifically, where do you want meekness to be seen in your life right now?

5
Hunger and Thirst

"Blessed are those who hunger and thirst for
righteousness,
for they will be filled."

Matthew 5:6

With this beatitude Jesus takes us a step further in our spiritual progression. Having seen our poverty of spirit and mourned over our sin and having become receptive to God's agenda, we now move from a more passive posture to a more active one—to earnestly seek God's way and his will. We seek to be filled with that which fills him.

As we consider hungering and thirsting, many of us have to ask ourselves if we can really comprehend what it means to be hungry, what it means to be thirsty.

We're not talking here about our stomach growling because it's time for lunch or our mid-afternoon snack. I can hear comments we tend to make echoing in my ears: "I'm dying for a _____ (something to eat or drink...you fill in the blank)." Or while standing in front of a full refrigerator: "There's nothing to eat/drink here!" Or "I'm starving!" We go into our favorite coffee shop and order a "for here, grande, nonfat, no water, 180°, chai tea latte."

Consider these comments in face of the staggering statistics on global hunger. Different websites report different numbers, but between 13,000 and 16,000 children are reported to die of starvation every day. Yes, that's right—every day. Our point is that it's hard for most of us to relate to the intensity, to the depth of desire that true hunger and thirst generate. The people of Jesus' day were perhaps more familiar with insecurity when it came to basic things such as food and drink. Their culture was more acquainted with real hunger and real thirst.

Perhaps it begins to come home to us when we hear of events such as the Andean plane crash as recounted in the book *Alive!* (later dramatized in the movie of the same name). People were driven to eat the flesh of their deceased companions in order to survive.

We may be horrified. But we have to grasp the intensity of the desire that we are talking about here. I don't remember where I (Steve) first heard it, but it really rings true: "God looks for you, not in your actions, but rather in your desires." And the question I have to ask myself is "What do I desire most?"

Do I really desire righteousness? Am I really that hungry? Am I really that thirsty? So much so that everything else pales in comparison with my desire for righteousness? We desire a lot of things. We want to be happy; we want to be satisfied. Even as we read these "Beatitudes," we can fall into the trap of desiring blessedness. Where we live, we often hear the expression "Have a blessed day!" What is it that we really want?

Desire for Righteousness

As we look at this specific beatitude, we can desire to be filled. But that's not what it says. The focus of our desire is not on the end result, which is definitely promised, but on what God wants us to be. What does "righteousness" really mean? Is it just doing the right actions? This is another one of those religious-sounding words that is seldom used in common speech. And whose righteousness are we talking about? Am I seeking my righteousness? No, in this kingdom message it has to be the righteousness of God.

Fred Faller's excellent study of righteousness in the Old Testament reveals that the word was more tied to the fulfillment of the relationship between two persons than to the fulfillment of a legalistic code.[1] The relationship was characterized by sharing, fairness, camaraderie and loyalty.

Stassen and Gushee point out that the Greek word for "righteousness," *dikaiosyne,* has the connotation of justice. They propose that Jesus could be referring to Isaiah 61, where three times Isaiah says that God is bringing righteousness and justice. *Tsedaqah* is the Hebrew word in Isaiah 61 which normally means delivering the kind of justice that rescues and releases oppressed people. The authors mention that they find Jesus confronting injustice forty times in the Gospels.

In the Old Testament "righteousness" means preserving the peace and wholeness of the community and is something parallel to *shalom.* So they conclude*: "...*in a nutshell, blessed are those who hunger and thirst for justice that delivers and restores the covenant community, for God is a God who brings such justice."[2]

To see the word "righteousness" as a religious word does not help us grasp its full impact. As we consider its use in the Old Testament, we see that it is primarily a relationship word. It is not about a set of rules; it is not about fulfilling ritual. It is primarily about building and honoring our relationships—first and foremost our relationship with God, then second our relationships with others.

So hungering and thirsting after righteousness is really about desiring a right relationship with God and with others. It is about digging deep and being faithful even when others are not faithful to us. God is faithful. God is righteous. He is our model.

Going Deeper

Perhaps the thoughts of a couple of scholars on this passage will heighten our understanding.

First, according to R.C.H. Lenski, we are dealing with a durative present participle.[3] This means we are not talking about a one-time thing but an ongoing process. When it comes to physical hunger this is obvious. Just because we ate a meal today doesn't mean that we are not going to have to eat again tomorrow.

We are talking about a day-in and day-out, lifelong pattern. If I read the Bible today, if I pray today, if I strive to live for God today and show his character, good! Tomorrow is another story.

Maybe that's why mountaintop spiritual experiences are often accompanied by times in the valley. It is like when you eat a really huge meal and then feel sluggish and tired afterwards. Then you don't sleep well that night and wake up still feeling uncomfortably full the next morning. Mountaintop times are awesome, but for real spiritual growth there's nothing like consistent times with the Lord.

Second, according to William Barclay, verbs of desire such as thirst and hunger generally occur with the genitive, but here they occur with the accusative. He says that the significance of this lies in wanting only a part (with the genitive) versus wanting the whole thing (with the accusative).[4] So how much "righteousness" do I want? Am I satisfied with just enough to make me look good? Do I want just enough to make me feel good? Or do I want it all? 100%. Everything that God has to offer.

Being Aware of Our Spiritual Condition

Perhaps it is important for us to consider here our own spiritual condition. Can you tell if you are spiritually dehydrated? If you are spiritually starving? Can you see the effects of missing a spiritual meal? I (Steve) don't do well when I don't eat on a regular basis. I'm pretty sensitive to whether

I have been fed or not, physically speaking. It is a lot harder to recognize the symptoms of spiritual need.

In light of this, we see the value of spiritual discipline. Regular helpings of Bible study, prayer, fellowship and public worship keep us on track. Special events, parallel to "eating out" can help us as well. Seminars, conferences, retreats, special times of fasting and prayer all play a part in seeing that we are well fed spiritually.

And what is the promise? "They will be filled." This is comforting. If we hunger and if we thirst for righteousness, then we will receive it. We will be filled. Like we said, God is always faithful. Our job is to focus on what we can do something about: our desire, our hunger, our thirst. We can be perfectly sure that God will do his job.

Questions for Study and Discussion

1. What do these two words—hunger and thirst—indicate about the kingdom life?
2. Why would you say this beatitude is the logical outgrowth of the first three?
3. What are some things "righteousness" doesn't mean and does mean?
4. What kinds of actions will you expect to see if one is hungering and thirsting for righteousness?
5. When such a person is filled, what would you expect to see?

6
The Merciful

"Blessed are the merciful,
    for they will be shown mercy."

Matthew 5:7

We all want to be shown mercy. We all want to be for-given in spite of our failings, our weaknesses and our sins. So as we turn to this beatitude, our attention naturally focuses first on God's mercy to us. This is an aspect of God that we like, that we approve of, because deep down inside, we all know that we need a gigantic helping of mercy.

One of the greatest attributes of God in Scripture is his mercy. We thrill with the beauty of the concept expressed in a passage such as Ephesians 2:4–5:

> ...but because of his great love for us, God, who is rich in mercy, made us alive with Christ even when we were dead in transgressions—it is by grace you have been saved.

We are drawn to those passages throughout the Bible that emphasize "but...God." No matter what happens, no matter how dire the circumstances, no matter how bad we mess up, those words are so reassuring. What God does always trumps whatever the world and the devil can throw at us.

Having just spoken about being filled up with God's righteousness, Jesus is now describing one of the chief characteristics of that righteousness: mercy. This reinforces what we have already said about the Sermon being rooted and grounded in grace. A key quality of the kingdom life is the abundance of mercy and grace.

Prayer for Mercy

Many of the references in the Bible to God's mercy are found in the context of prayer as men poured their hearts out to God pleading with him for mercy. For example in 1 Chronicles 21:13 we find David speaking: "I am in deep distress. Let me fall into the hands of the Lord, for his mercy is very great." Over and over again in the Psalms we find these expressions "Be merciful to me, God" or "Have mercy on me, Lord."

On a personal level, both of us find the phrase: "Lord, have mercy!" coming to our lips almost involuntarily when we are particularly tired or feeling a lot of stress. It is a very natural prayer to pray in situations when we're in over our heads. The writings of the Psalms would strongly indicate that God welcomes those prayers.

Our Mercy Toward Others

The first focus of this beatitude, however, is not on the mercy that God extends to us but rather the mercy that we extend to others. According to this beatitude, God's continued mercy is the result of our action. When we responded to the first two beatitudes, we already experienced God's mercy and grace. We saw ourselves as we are; we were distressed over our sin; we humbled ourselves before God; we harnessed the desire to be right with him and others. So even before our response to this beatitude, we are already walking in his grace and living by his mercy. This beatitude calls us to live continually in the mercy we have already received.

When Jesus pronounced a blessing on the merciful, he was definitely not in tune with the thinking of the world in his day. In the Roman world, pity was despised. Compassion was considered a vice. Children who were born sickly or weak were often disposed of, left outside to die.

Although Jesus' blessing on the merciful was not in tune with the practice of the world around him, it definitely was in tune with the need of the world and the description of the promised Kingdom in the Old Testament (Isaiah 63:9).

Alvin J. Schmidt in his book, *How Christianity Changed the World,* argues that the compassion and mercy of the Christians was the origin of hospitals and healthcare as we know it, as well as orphanages and concern for the elderly and many other benevolent actions.[1]

What does this have to do with you and me? The Parable of the Unmerciful Servant that Jesus told in Matthew 18:23–35 perfectly clarifies our role in this process. We have received mercy so that we can extend mercy. If we don't extend mercy then it will be taken away from us. We are the $10 million debtors (our approximate monetary equivalent of 10,000 talents). So what are we going to do? How are we going to treat the guy who owes us a few dollars?

Temptation to Look Down on Others

Looking at the connection with the previous beatitudes, we see that one of the dangers of spiritual growth and realization is to look down on others rather than consider them with mercy and compassion. If I am hungering and thirsting for righteousness, then it might become easy for me to look down on those who are not. I might find myself judging others based on my own achievements, so Jesus tells us the next step is to extend mercy, to have mercy, to be merciful.

The truth is that when a passion for righteousness is not combined with compassion and mercy, horrible things happen. Jesus was dealing with this very issue in many of his interactions with the Pharisees. This is why we continue to stress that these beatitudes are all ongoing in nature. We never arrive. We always have room for growth, for improvement. We always have to keep going back to the first beatitude.

One of the areas where we see this principle running head on into reality is in our ability, or our willingness to forgive others. Supposedly mature disciples, with years in the faith, struggle to let go of past hurts and injuries. Somehow we seem to think that because emotional damage was done in a spiritual context, we are justified in holding on to our hurts. Sadly in this case the beatitude proves true: When we refuse to extend mercy, we stop receiving mercy. We have seen many individuals walk away from their faith in God because of their unwillingness to forgive.

Evangelistic Beatitude

To take it to another level, this principle of extending mercy may be the first time in these beatitudes that Jesus specifically directs our attention toward those on the outside. This is the first evangelistic beatitude. I've got to pass on to others the mercy that has been extended to me. I want other people to know what God is doing in our world.

We can remember a little song we sang when we were teenagers called, "Love Is Something if You Give It Away." That's the way it is with mercy. Here is the fascinating truth: Try to hoard God's mercy, and like Israel's manna in the desert, you will lose it. But keep letting it fill you and overflow from you and just run all over the place, almost wastefully, and it will keep coming back to you in a never-ending cycle.

As we have said, when people come to God they come to one who is "rich in mercy." In a corporate sense, when people come to us (the church), they are coming to God's people. What do they find? People rich in mercy? Or people quick to judge and condemn?

Something we have to be clear about is that mercy is not moral turpitude; it is not to cause us to be morally wishy-washy or to "take it easy" on sin. God makes that perfectly clear in sending his own Son to pay the price for our sin. Mercy is born out of incredible sacrifice.

God's Forgiveness

So does that mean that God's forgiveness is conditional upon my mercy? In other words, if I forgive others, then God has to forgive me. Hardly. As we have seen in these beatitudes, God's forgiveness and mercy is extended as we realize our need for him and humble ourselves before him. However, if at any point along the way, we refuse to extend mercy to others, then we are by that very act rejecting God's grace and mercy.

When the apostle Paul closes out the first eleven chapters of his letter to the Romans, he ends it with a section of praise to God for his incredible wisdom and knowledge. He begins chapter 12 with a challenge for us to lay our lives down in sacrifice. As he does he reminds us that we do this "in view of God's mercy." J. B. Phillips translates it beautifully: "with eyes wide open to the mercies of God" (Romans 12:1). This is the challenge we face every day—to keep our eyes fixed on the incredible mercy of God so that we are capable of extending mercy to those around us.

As noted earlier, no New Testament book echoes more phrases from the Sermon than the letter of James, so mistakenly misunderstood by Luther as a book that did not really contain the gospel. On this beatitude we allow James to help us close the chapter:

> Speak and act as those who are going to be judged
> by the law that gives freedom, because judgment
> without mercy will be shown to anyone who has not
> been merciful. Mercy triumphs over judgment!
> (James 2:12–13)

Want a picture of kingdom life? It is a place where mercy triumphs over judgment!

Questions for Study and Discussion

1. Why will a person who has moved through the first four beatitudes feel he or she has received a gigantic portion of mercy?
2. How do you expect that seeking to live the message of the Sermon will cause you to see your need for mercy again and again?
3. If we are being filled with God's righteousness, how will mercy toward others be seen in our lives?
4. What effect will demonstrating mercy have in the lives of people—in a family, in a church, in the world?
5. Are you known as one who is merciful?

7
The Pure in Heart

"Blessed are the pure in heart,
for they will see God."

Matthew 5:8

Let's review again. We are poor in spirit—we see ourselves as we are—and we receive the Kingdom. Then we
mourn—we hurt over what our sin has done—and we are
comforted. Third, we become meek—we humble ourselves
before God and accept his will—and thus begin the process
by which we inherit the earth. We hunger and thirst—we
intensely desire to be right with God and others—and so we
are filled. This brings us to the first beatitude that really turns
outward, that focuses on our actions toward others. At this
point we are very aware of the mercy that we have received
from God and so we are motivated to want to share this
mercy with others.

So as we travel down this path, this walk with God, at

this point it seems that two temptations can come to our hearts: (1) We experience disappointment and frustration as we strive to live this life and share God's grace with others. We respond by getting bitter, angry or depressed (depending on our particular sinful nature). Or (2) We experience success as we live this life and share God's grace with others and get prideful and full of self. "Woohoo! Look what I did!"

Whichever happens to us, the solution is the same. Go back to square one, back to the beginning. See myself as I am, recognize and hurt over the state of my heart, humble myself before God and seek his mercy, strive intensely to maintain my connection with him, become refilled and go back to sharing that mercy with others.

Pure Motivations

So this brings us to Jesus' words: "Blessed are the pure in heart." To continue on the journey, we have to deal with our hearts. We must be sure that we are focused on the right things for the right reasons, that our motivations are pure.

Now let's take a deeper look at this verse. What is the meaning of "pure in heart"? The Greek word for "pure" is used in a variety of contexts: (1) of dirty clothes that have been washed—"clean"; (2) of corn or grain after the chaff is sifted out—"purified"; (3) of metal that has all the impurities removed—"unadulterated"; (4) of an army cleared of all the cowards and lazy and malcontents—"purged." The essence of pure in heart seems to come down to one central thought expressed in various ways: single-minded, free from the tyranny of a divided self, unmixed motives, no hidden motives, no selfish interests. Soren Kierkegaard had a great title for one of his books: *Purity of Heart Is to Will One Thing.*

Religion tends to travel down one of three paths. Consider the following delineation.

First: a focus on intellect, the pursuit of knowledge or enlightenment. D. Martyn Lloyd-Jones said, "When people have had only an intellectual interest in these matters it has oftentimes been a curse to the church."[1] Paul referred in 2 Timothy 3:7 to those who are "ever learning, and never able to come to the knowledge of the truth. (ASV)"

Second: a focus on behavior, characterized in Jesus' day by a group like the Pharisees. Note Jesus' emphasis in Matthew 23:25–26:

> "...You clean the outside of the cup and dish, but inside they are full of greed and self-indulgence! Blind Pharisee! First clean the inside of the cup, so the outside of it may also become clean."

Third: a focus on emotions. So much of today's religion is characterized by this emphasis, guided by passions (2 Timothy 3:6) or by instinct (Jude 10). Paul described misled people who were emotionally based in these words:

> Such a person goes into great detail about what he has seen, and his unspiritual mind puffs him up with idle notions. (Colossians 2:18)

Jesus emphasized a fourth path. Without discounting the importance of the intellect, behavior or emotions, throughout his ministry he always brought us back to the centrality of "heart" in all we are and do (e.g., Matthew 5:28; 6:2; 15:8, 18; Luke 6:45), but never so clearly as in this passage we are studying in this chapter.

Heart Versus Emotions

But some will ask, "Isn't 'heart' the same as 'emotions'?" This is a common misconception, and it is obvious that emotions have something to do with heart. However, if you will reflect on how the word is used in other spheres, it makes the delineation more clear. In the athletic realm, for example, when we say someone plays with "heart," we mean that they play with a great deal of determination and willpower. Yes, emotion is a part of it, but not the most essential part.

So how do I know what is in my heart? To be honest, this is where it can get a bit scary. Let me (Steve) speak from personal experience in the physical realm. For many years my blood pressure was borderline high. I kept it in check by watching my weight and by running. When I was paralyzed on the left side by MS, I was no longer able to run as I had before, and so I was forced to begin taking blood pressure medication. The thing about high blood pressure is that it generally has no symptoms. Most of the time you have no idea if it is high or low, although with experience you learn that high stress levels often transmit to high blood pressure.

A few years later, after finding a substitute for running

(cycling with a friend, Kevin Frantz, on a tandem bike), I found myself in pretty good shape. In addition to biking, I worked out in the gym. Kevin and I even competed in a few state time-trial events on the bike.

One day while on a hike with my wife, Diane, I noticed that I was especially tired and feeling a little pressure in my chest. I talked it over with my physician and friend, John Scott, and he made an appointment for me to see a cardiologist immediately.

Although nothing showed up on the standard tests, the cardiologist recommended an angiogram to see if anything was wrong. It turned out there was a lot wrong! Several arteries were almost completely blocked. The doctors refused to let me leave the hospital and kept me over the weekend so open-heart surgery could be performed on Monday.

You see, that's what's scary. You could have something very wrong inside of you even though on the outside everything seems to be fine. All that to say this: The only way I could know what was really in my heart was to get outside help—to literally have someone look and see. It would be great if spiritual "heart doctors" were able to do the same thing, but God has not left us without help.

Getting in Touch with Our Heart

The tools that God gives us to be able to analyze our hearts are first and foremost the Word, prayer and relationships with others. So if we're going to have hearts that are pure, we need to avail ourselves of all of these helps.

When I was in college I heard a minister, Jim Woodruff, share these questions to help evaluate the purity of our hearts.

1. What are your pleasures? Do you take pleasure in praise? In self-display? In prestige? Do you like to feel superior to others?
2. What are your treasures?
3. Whom do you try to please?
4. Why do you live?

The answers to these should drive us back to the first beatitude. They drive us to our knees because it's so obvious that we are often poorly or wrongly motivated, and so weak and so helpless without him.

Healthy Heart

So what do I do about the state of my heart? Well, let's go back to the physical parallels: How do I keep my heart in good shape? Diet is obviously important, physically speaking. So how is your spiritual diet? What are you feeding your soul?

Exercise is valuable. I have to push myself to go to the gym and get the physical exercise I need. In the spiritual realm we also have to push ourselves. It takes effort. It takes discipline. And consistency is the most important factor.

And last but not least—I need additional help. I need medication to keep blood pressure and cholesterol regulated. So I have to schedule regular doctor visits. We all need help spiritually as well—additional, personal and regular help so that we can stay in touch with our hearts.

That is why I sometimes need to sit down and have a heart-to-heart with my wife, talk through what we are doing and what we want to do and how we are feeling about it. Or I have to pick up the phone and call a brother (more often than not it is Tom) and share what I'm feeling, get stuff out in the open so I can see more clearly what is going on in my heart.

The promise connected with being pure in heart is that we will see God. So when do we get to see God? According to Colossians 1:15, we see him in Jesus: "The Son is the image of the invisible God." Jesus is for us God in the flesh. We see him in the universe as we gaze upon the beauty God has created here on this earth, as we contemplate the splendor of the nighttime sky that unfolds before us. We also can see God in our own personal history. As we look back on the twists and turns of our lives, in retrospect we can see God's touch here and there and there again.

And one day, we believe with all our hearts we will see him face to face.

Questions for Study and Discussion

1. How would you define a pure heart?
2. What are some of the greatest challenges of keeping a pure heart?
3. What do we need in order to be in touch with what is really in our hearts?
4. What is the import of David's statement in Psalm 51:10, and how have you found it to be true?
5. What decisions will you make to keep seeking a pure heart?

8
The Peacemakers

"Blessed are the peacemakers
for they will be called sons of God."

Matthew 5:9

We pointed out in Volume One of our study on the Kingdom that when Isaiah speaks of the coming reign of God, he emphasizes the theme of peace as much as justice and righteousness. In the Kingdom, swords will be beaten into farming implements (Isaiah 2:4), and natural enemies will live together (Isaiah 11:5–9). The one who is coming will be called the Prince of Peace, and his government and peace will have no end (Isaiah 9:6–7).

Since Jesus' message is that the Kingdom Isaiah looked forward to has come and has broken into the present age, it is no surprise to find in these crucial Beatitudes that kingdom people will be makers of peace, not makers of war. As they do God's will on earth "as it is in heaven," peace will be a vital concern.

What Is Peace?

But what is peace? The word in Greek is *eirene* and means "tranquility." It is used to describe a boat sailing on a calm sea. It denotes harmony and describes a song in which all notes and chords blend in perfect agreement. It conveys the idea of an absence of strife, calling to mind two people walking hand in hand along the road.

The English word "peace" comes from Latin *pax,* which has to do with a pact or treaty between two parties.

But more important to us in this study is the Hebrew word for "peace," which was *shalom,* a word still important to modern Jews. Not only does *shalom* convey the passive— the absence of strife and evil—but also the active, the presence of all good things. To wish *shalom* on another was in essence to say, "I wish for you not only the absence of all that may harm but also the presence of everything that makes for your good."

While our instinct is to assume that we are talking about peace between people, we should consider whether this is the first place to go. In Isaiah 27:5, the prophet has God speaking these words:

> "Or else let them come to me for refuge;
>   let them make peace with me,
>   yes, let them make peace with me."

The peace that needs to be made in this passage first is peace with God. Later on in Isaiah 59:1–2, God will describe how the people's sins have brought about a separation be-

tween God and them. But prior to that in Isaiah 53:5, he had
described the suffering servant as one who would be
"pierced for our transgressions" and "crushed for our iniqui-
ties" so that "the punishment that brought us peace was
upon him." In context this very much sounds like he was
bringing peace with God.

If we look back at the Beatitudes, we can make a strong
case for the fact that the first four beatitudes are all about
coming to peace, first of all, with God. When we put all of
this in a broader New Testament context, looking at passages such as Romans 5:1, Ephesians 2:13–18 and 2 Corinthians 5:18–20, we can see that "peace with God" or being
reconciled to God is the greatest concern. And we can see
that peace with God then becomes the key to peace in all
other relationships.

Helping Others Find Peace with God

It may very well be that the first four beatitudes deal primarily with our relationship with God and that the second
four deal with our relationships with other people, which
would put this beatitude in the second category But there
can be no real peacemaking among people without a concern to bring them first to peace with God. Shortly, Jesus
will be talking about loving our enemies, but who has any
hope of doing that if he does not have a relationship with
God that gives him power beyond himself?

So here would be our take on this beatitude: *In many
ways we might call it the supreme or overtly evangelistic*

beatitude. Jesus is calling us to share the good news of the Kingdom with others so that they might first of all find peace with God. Then they will have a reason to beat their swords into plowshares and a reason to love and come together with those they have seen as enemies.

We cannot believe that Jesus is telling us to wait until we see a fight breaking out and then try to get between the people and negotiate a peace, although a disciple might very well do that. Jesus is calling us, to use Paul's words, to be "ministers of reconciliation" and to urge people, whatever their current condition, to "be reconciled to God." Now, of course, the way we do this is to teach them the previous beatitudes and call them to the kind of repentance those beatitudes describe.

When people have been reconciled to God, they will have a transformed life that causes them to want reconciliation and peace with others. It also motivates them to call other people to be reconciled and have peace with each other.

Not Necessarily Popular

We might think people would welcome and appreciate peacemakers. But remember Jeremiah's statement about those who don't really deal with the issues: "They say, 'Peace, peace,' when there is no peace. They heal the wound of my people superficially." This is what most people want. They don't want to face their sin because to do so would bring pain. They just want two piña coladas and a few laughs. To bring people to peace with God we need to help them have poverty of spirit, to mourn over their sin, and to be meek and humble before God. We all know not everyone welcomes this call to change. Your neighbor may enjoy your company but only as long as you don't challenge his life in some way.

Jesus was the Prince of Peace described by Isaiah, but we see what happened to him. He did not gloss over people's deeper problems. He was the doctor who told people the truth about their condition. It takes great conviction to hunger and thirst for righteousness. It takes great compassion to be merciful. It takes great courage and love to be a peacemaker. One has to be secure in his or her own peace with God and not dependent on the reactions of others for personal worth or security. Peacemakers are a bit like professional baseball players—even the good ones have fairly low batting averages or low percentages of success.

How far did peacemaking lead Jesus, and how far should we go? The writer of Hebrews says,

> And so Jesus also suffered outside the city gate to make the people holy through his own blood. Let us, then, go to him outside the camp, bearing the disgrace he bore.

In order to be the Prince of Peace, Jesus also had to be the Suffering Servant, one who went outside the city gate to be disgraced. But the writer's words let us know that we cannot say, "Thank God we won't have to do that," for he calls us to go to him outside the city gate and share in his sufferings. As I (Tom) once heard my friend Larry Craig preach, this is a call for us to go outside the camps of our comfort, convenience, complacency and cowardice. We cannot be peacemakers who bring people to God if we stay in the safety of our camps.

Peace with Others

Most of what we have said so far is about bringing people to peace with God, but certainly we must be equally passionate about bringing people to peace with each other. We just have to get first things first. Jesus will soon be talking about our responsibility to seek reconciliation with those who have something against us.

One of Jesus' last and most fervent prayers was for the unity of believers. Paul's letters abound with statements about resolving conflicts and working for unity. Inherent in the gospel message and the Beatitudes themselves are principles that will bring people together, and kingdom people are called to relentlessly apply these principles.

This beatitude is calling every disciple in the Kingdom to be a peacemaker, but we cannot help others unless we are vigilant about working out our relationships with others in the body of Christ. If we are harboring bitterness or resentment or hurt feelings toward another disciple, we must be urgent about getting help. Such unresolved relationships will keep us from being people who bring peace.

Do Christians have a responsibility to work for peace in the wider world? The answer must certainly be that we should work for peace in every setting possible because hatred, distrust, strife and violence are never God's will. If we have the opportunity to help our neighbors with their marriage or to influence people we work with to stop hating those of another race or another nation, we should seize the moment. But we should see all such opportunities as occasions to declare the gospel of the Kingdom and never be content to use worldly or superficial means of trying to create peace, though they be more palatable.

Even though we may start out just helping people listen and understand each other, we should be looking for opportunities to take the conversations to a deeper level so we can introduce others to the gospel of peace.

Later on we will come to Jesus' teaching about loving our enemies and praying for them and doing good to them. How often do people come into our churches and hear prayers for our enemies? Would that not communicate a greater passion for peace? Maybe that does not happen often because in our own private prayers we are not praying for our enemies. If we're looking for a positive step to take to be peacemakers, this would seem to be a right place to begin. Of course, if you find your heart is not in it, let that drive you back to the first beatitude where you can once again seek God's mercy and transforming power.

Sons of God

Why will those who are peacemakers be called the sons of God? They are doing God's work in the world. They have the same passion that God has. He wants to bring all things together, and certainly all people together, in Christ (Colossians 1:19–20).

At Jesus' baptism, the heavens opened and God said, "This is my Son in whom I am well pleased." Jesus did not become God's Son there at his baptism, but by virtue of Jesus' action, God was saying in so many words, "That's my boy!"

When we go outside the camp and lay our lives down to be peacemakers, we enter into the work of God, and God says, "That's my girl!" or "That's my boy!"

Questions for Study and Discussion

1. In the context of the other beatitudes why does it make sense to say that helping others to have peace with God is the first order of business for the peacemaker?
2. Why will peacemaking involve helping others understand the six beatitudes that come before this one?
3. What kind of peace are we seeking to bring among people?
4. What are the implications of this beatitude for those who find themselves in church conflicts? In conflicts in the community? In conflicts among nations? What attitudes do we often see in these settings that are in great conflict with the Kingdom?
5. What price did Jesus pay to be a peacemaker, and what price are you willing to pay?

9
Those Who Are Persecuted

"Blessed are those who are persecuted because of
righteousness,
for theirs is the kingdom of heaven."
Matthew 5:10

Perhaps you have heard the saying that "no good deed goes unpunished." The person who internalizes the first seven beatitudes may find that this indeed is true. We have here a person who has humbled himself before God, then has become broken and contrite over his sin, receptive and teachable, hungry for righteousness, full of mercy toward other people, all the while working to keep his own heart pure. And in a world of conflict he is committed to being a peacemaker. And what does he get for all of this? Persecution!

Hatred! The anger and disapproval of the very ones he is seeking to help!

This is the way Jesus closes out the Beatitudes:

> "Blessed are those who are persecuted because of righteousness,
>   for theirs is the kingdom of heaven.
>
> "Blessed are you when people insult you, persecute you and falsely say all kinds of evil against you because of me. Rejoice and be glad, because great is your reward in heaven, for in the same way they persecuted the prophets who were before you." (Matthew 5:10–12)

There is good news and bad news here. The bad news is the world will not generally appreciate this wonderful new life that you have. The good news is you're on the right side (of history and eternity) and you can rejoice about this and celebrate your place in the Kingdom.

It is not that Jesus wants to end the Beatitudes on a negative note; he just ends them on a truthful note. *Age-to-come living in this present age is going to be so "other worldly" that it will rub many the wrong way, and Jesus simply tells it like it is.* All the other beatitudes are qualities we must allow God to produce in us; this one describes what happens to us when we live out those qualities. No one can ever accuse Jesus of hiding anything in the fine print. He made it clear from the beginning how kingdom values will clash with those of the world.

Peter is the one who will later describe the members of God's holy nation as aliens and strangers in this world (1 Peter 2:11). As disciples live conscious that their citizenship is in heaven and they are under the reign of God, they will seem to be, as the King James Version translates it, "a peculiar people" (1 Peter 2:9).

While it is true in general that kingdom people will live a life that makes them seem quite strange to those around them, it strikes us that the seventh beatitude, which immediately precedes this one, is the real sticking point and produces the strongest reactions. If disciples were to develop these internal qualities but just kept to themselves, as some groups are known to do, they might be regarded as a bit odd but would escape any serious opposition.

However, when they call those around them to make peace with God in his Kingdom, trouble often begins. As we pointed out in the last chapter, many people do not want to be confronted with their sin even though the message of Jesus promises them a real deliverance from it.

In our experience it is when we are most aggressively (but still humbly) sharing the good news of the Kingdom and calling people to "repent"—to look to the age to come for direction—that we have seen the most opposition.

It is interesting that Jesus devotes more comments to this matter of persecution than he does to any of the other topics we have looked at. He makes it clear that opposition is coming and that many false accusations will be made against kingdom people. Since this is the way it is, he urges his disciples to rejoice in the face of it, knowing that the same thing happened in the past when the prophets brought God's truth to the people.

A Consistent Message

With all the beatitudes we have tried to see how their message is repeated in the remainder of the New Testament. We don't have to go far to hear words like these being spoken again to the followers of Jesus. In Matthew 10:21–24 we find this statement from Jesus:

> "Brother will betray brother to death, and a father his child; children will rebel against their parents and have them put to death. All men will hate you because of me, but he who stands firm to the end will be saved. When you are persecuted in one place, flee to another. I tell you the truth, you will not finish going through the cities of Israel before the Son of Man comes. A student is not above his teacher, nor a servant above his master."

Just a few verses later, Jesus gives another warning tinged with a bit of irony:

> "Do not suppose that I have come to bring peace to the earth. I did not come to bring peace, but a sword. For I have come to turn
>
> "'a man against his father,
>   a daughter against her mother,

> a daughter-in-law against her mother-in-law—
>> a man's enemies will be the members of
>>> his own household.'"
> (Matthew 10:34–36)

Jesus was the Prince of Peace and not a man of the sword, but his call to make him Lord and live by the principles of his Kingdom cuts through the unity of families, so that loving your enemy often eventually meant loving your relatives.

In the Gospel of John the words of Jesus are even more specific:

> "If the world hates you, keep in mind that it hated me first. If you belonged to the world, it would love you as its own. As it is, you do not belong to the world, but I have chosen you out of the world. That is why the world hates you. Remember the words I spoke to you: 'No servant is greater than his master.' If they persecuted me, they will persecute you also. If they obeyed my teaching, they will obey yours also." (John 15:18–20)

In this passage Jesus gives the fundamental reason for opposition: Disciples no longer belong to this world. They take their direction from another place. There are some "ifs" in this passage, but when we read "if they persecuted me, they will persecute you also," we realize we aren't being given some wiggle room. Their persecution of him was a fact, and so it will happen to his disciples.

The type of opposition that kingdom people will receive will vary from country to country or culture to culture and from time to time. However, if we live what we believe to be a kingdom life year after year and never experience opposition, insult or injury because of our faith, doesn't it mean that something in our "faith" experience must be missing? Doesn't it mean that we can hardly be distinguished from the world, or at least from the religious world? This would seem to be true, especially in light of Paul's words: "In fact, everyone who wants to live a godly life in Christ Jesus will be persecuted" (2 Timothy 3:12).

Continue to Examine Our Hearts

As we go further into the Sermon, we are likely to find some unpopular teachings that we may have avoided because embracing them not only would be difficult for us but would cause others to more forcefully criticize us. We must be ready to examine our hearts and more faithfully obey.

Surely it goes without saying that if we are not receiving opposition or criticism that we should not go out and seek it. We are called to seek the Kingdom and his righteousness, never to seek persecution. However, receiving no opposition certainly presents an opportunity to examine our lives.

We know well that Christians can be persecuted for unrighteousness as well as for righteousness. Peter had to address this in 1 Peter 4:12–16. The sad truth is that some Christians have been spoken against because of being rude, disrespectful, inconsiderate or self-righteous. Others have been opposed because of exhibiting racism or nationalism. Negative reactions have come because of the way we have abused certain biblical concepts related to authority or relationships. When this happens, there's nothing to rejoice about because the gospel has been distorted and disfigured.

Jesus' words in the Beatitudes make it clear that opposition/persecution for righteousness' sake becomes an opportunity to rejoice. It also becomes an opportunity to return good for evil, again something that sadly has often not been done. It becomes an opportunity to shine even brighter, and this is where Jesus will take us in the next verses we will consider.

Yours Is the Kingdom

We cannot, however, leave this text without observing that the promise made to those who are persecuted is the same promise made at the beginning to those who are poor in spirit: "Yours is the kingdom." At the beginning it's about the Kingdom, and at the end it's about the Kingdom.

The Kingdom is populated by spiritual beggars who get trashed by the world, but they rejoice because they have found the pearl of great price and the treasure hidden in the field. They know him who has the words of eternal life.

Questions for Study and Discussion

1. Why does something that sounds like such bad news show up at the very end of the beatitudes?
2. Why do you think the New Testament seems to assume that persecution will be inevitable for those who live the kingdom life?
3. What are your honest feelings about persecution? Do you fear it? Seek to avoid it? Dread it?
4. How is Jesus seeking to help us see persecution not as just a negative?
5. How is your living the kingdom life bringing you or your church persecution?

10
Salt and Light

We tend to think that Jesus' comments about persecution are the closing words of the Beatitudes. However, as we have come to understand it, the words that come after these comments are a continuation of his thoughts on the Beatitudes as they are a description of the impact people's lives will have as they live the Beatitudes. Here is what he says:

> "You are the salt of the earth. But if the salt loses its saltiness, how can it be made salty again? It is no longer good for anything, except to be thrown out and trampled by men.
> "You are the light of the world. A city on a hill cannot be hidden. Neither do people light a lamp and put it under a bowl. Instead they put it on its stand, and it gives light to everyone in the house. In the same way, let your light shine before men, that

they may see your good deeds and praise your Father in heaven." (Matthew 5:13–16)

Jesus chooses two metaphors that would have quickly connected with his hearers. Salt was such an extremely valuable commodity that the ancients spoke of routes of commerce as "salt routes," indicating that this transport was the most important purpose of the routes. Today we are familiar with wars being fought over oil rights. In much the same way, wars were fought over salt in that day. Of course, the metaphor of light is timeless.

The first obvious idea from both images is that the disciples living this age-to-come life will not be pulling away from society and retreating to isolated communities. To accomplish their purposes both salt and light have to penetrate, in the first case, the meat, and in the second case, the darkness.

Though disciples of Jesus will be living as those with their "citizenship in heaven" (Philippians 3:20), as subjects of God's government (his Kingdom), they will be penetrating society just as Jesus did. The age to come will be breaking into the present through their lives (see figure 2).

Let's take a more careful look at the two metaphors Jesus uses.

Salt Metaphor

Salt was primarily used as a preservative to keep meat from decomposing in days before refrigeration. Rubbing salt into the meat allowed it to be stored or transported and be

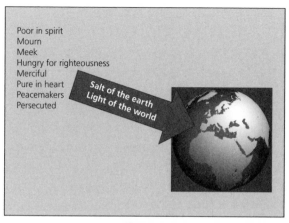

Poor in spirit
Mourn
Meek
Hungry for righteousness
Merciful
Pure in heart
Peacemakers
Persecuted

Salt of the earth
Light of the world

Figure 2

edible for an extended period. The importance of this use can hardly be overemphasized. When armies would go on campaigns and needed rations, salt was the only way that meat could be preserved. An army devoid of salt was an army that was weakening. As recently as the Civil War in the United States, armies were put in desperate situations because of the lack of salt.

Salt was also used for healing purposes, especially for dealing with infections, much as it is today. Many of us have had a dentist extract a tooth and then tell us to rinse that area several times a day with warm salt water.

Then, as today, salt would have been used to add flavor to food. While it is possible that Jesus had all these usages in mind, it is most likely that the preservative nature of salt was the main concept he wanted to communicate.

So it would seem Jesus is saying that kingdom people who live with the aforementioned kingdom attitudes will offer hope to a rotting world. They may look like a ragtag group. They might not have any impressive credentials in the world's eyes. They may appear to be the picture of ordinariness. However, as they penetrate the world, they will make an impact. They will be persecuted by some, but others will see the truth of their message and will respond. Instead of rotting away in a futile life, these few who decide to seek the Kingdom will be transformed into people with eternity in their hearts.

Jesus does add a warning to his disciples: "If the salt loses its saltiness, how can it be made salty again? It is no longer good for anything except to be thrown out and trampled by men." Salt makes a difference because it is distinctive. If it loses its distinctiveness and becomes like what it is trying to preserve, you might as well throw it out. It goes from being essential to being useless. If we water down the message of Jesus, if we become like so many who avoid, rationalize or compromise his strong teachings, we will lose our distinctiveness and will make no difference in the world. This is why we must keep going back to the Beatitudes and then approach the rest of the Sermon with a heart that wants to fully obey—not evade.

We should point out here that the phrase "They are the salt of the earth" has become popular to describe something different from what Jesus has in mind. To say that John and Mary are the salt of the earth is to say what good, decent, hard-working, down-to-earth people they are. They are the kind of people everybody just has to like and appreciate; they are real pillars of the community.

There is much right about being decent and hard-working, but the people Jesus describes will not be liked by all people. Remember verse 13 immediately follows verses 10-12. These salt-of-the-earth kingdom people may be intensely disliked. Things they say may sting and burn like salt on a wound. We must not confuse distinctive kingdom living with "niceness."

While talking about how salt can sting, it seems a good place to mention a comment made by Helmut Thielicke, the European theologian. He said, "I'm afraid a lot of Christians are more interested in being the honey of the world than the salt of the earth." He went on to observe that being honey will probably mean you will be liked and will make some people feel good. However, honey does not preserve. Salt does.

Light Metaphor

The other metaphor that Jesus uses is light—one of the most common used to characterize the value of spiritual life. By living the Beatitudes in a world usually characterized by their opposites, disciples bring light into the darkness, exposing sin so that it can be seen for what it is and revealing the true way people are to relate to God and to one another.

By saying that disciples are the light of the world, Jesus is making a statement about the condition of the world: It is in darkness. We don't live in the Dark Ages, or do we? We live in the age of space travel with people already making reservations for space-trip vacations. We live in the age of computers. We both are using voice recognition software to write much of this book (very nice for guys with MS). Most of you have a device in your pocket or purse that enables you to make a call, send a text, post something on Facebook and watch the game of your choice.

But don't be naïve. We live in the darkness. People don't know God. They aren't humble before him. They live to please themselves. Children are abused by religious leaders. The courts are full of lawsuits. Smart bombs kill women and children. The sexualization of young girls is seen everywhere. Church people avoid the poor. Millions are enslaved to Internet porn. Politicians are caught in affairs left and right soon after announcing a platform of family values. But the Kingdom of God can break into this darkness, exposing it and showing the way, the truth and the life.

Into the darkness will come new ways of conducting relationships; new ways of handling sexuality; serious commitments to lifelong marriages; out-of-this-world ways to respond to evil, aggression and force; a mind-blowing love for enemies; a disengagement from the culture of consumerism; an end to hypocritical judgmentalism; and a confidence in a God who cares for us much more than we care for our own children. This is all about a new world being lived in the midst of an old one. This light is shining in a dark place.

Here again there are some common phrases that must not be confused with what Jesus is talking about. We may say that Claudia just lights up a room when she walks in. It is nice to have people like this who brighten up our lives. However, Jesus is not describing people with vivacious personalities. He is describing those who live with a consciousness of God that comes through in their actions and shines light on all kinds of situations.

If you stop and reflect on where we started in the first beatitude and what Jesus is saying to us now, you see something quite remarkable. Those who start out confessing their poverty of spirit, those saying to God, "Have mercy on me, for I am a spiritual beggar with no righteousness of my own," are now being told, "You are the salt of the earth and the light of the world; you are the hope of hundreds and thousands."

Can we sing a few verses of "Amazing Grace"? This is the good news of the Kingdom. Those who humbly admit their need and place whatever they have under the rule and reign of God will be those used by God to change the lives of those around them—by showing them the same road that starts at the beginning beatitude.

Questions for Study and Discussion

1. How is it helpful to see the statements about being salt and light as really the conclusion of the thoughts about the Beatitudes?
2. What are your thoughts about this quote: "I'm afraid a lot of Christians are more interested in being the honey of the world than the salt of the earth"? What is the difference?
3. How can we be fooled into thinking that our world is not really in darkness?
4. What is the evidence that we are in fact in a dark world?
5. How will living the Beatitudes bring light into people's lives?
6. Which is more true: (1) We are salt and light individually or (2) We are salt and light collectively?

11
Kingdom Righteousness

"Do not think that I have come to abolish the Law or the Prophets; I have not come to abolish them but to fulfill them. I tell you the truth, until heaven and earth disappear, not the smallest letter, not the least stroke of a pen [not an iota or a dot—ESV], will by any means disappear from the Law until everything is accomplished. Anyone who breaks one of the least of these commandments and teaches others to do the same will be called least in the kingdom of heaven, but whoever practices and teaches these commands will be called great in the kingdom of heaven. For I tell you that unless your righteousness surpasses that of the Pharisees and the teachers of the law, you will certainly not enter the kingdom of heaven."   Matthew 5:17–20

As we continue our study, we are seeing the dynamic aspect of the Kingdom unfold. It is God's rule, God's reign in our hearts and lives. As Jesus said, it is not "here" or "there" (Luke 17:20–21), but the temptation has always been to reduce the Kingdom to something tangible that we can grasp (both mentally and physically). We want it to be something that we can hold on to, such as "our church" or "heaven" to give two examples. The nature of the Kingdom is dynamic and active—God, first through Jesus and now through us, is breaking into our universe, our time and place, changing *us* and thus changing our world.

The Beatitudes set forth the standard for living the kingdom life, which when lived, makes an impact in the lives of the people around us. As we move on into this message, we are going to consider some key underlying principles that Jesus will expound upon.

Matthew 5:17–18 is a challenging passage, but it would not be here if it was not important and related to all we are learning about the Kingdom of God. When we first started studying in earnest to prepare for the series that we preached in Nashville, I called Tom one morning scratching my head and asking him, "What is your take on 17–20? It has really got me confused." Then as we set the schedule for who would teach which passages, I wound up with this one. However, I love to study the Bible, to dig in and really try to hear what the Lord wants me to hear. So, let's do that right now.

Going Deeper

> "Do not think that I have come to abolish the Law or the Prophets; I have not come to abolish them but to fulfill them. I tell you the truth, until heaven and earth disappear, not the smallest letter, not the least stroke of a pen [not an iota or a dot—ESV], will by any means disappear from the Law until everything is accomplished." (vv17–18)

The first understanding we can clearly grasp is that Jesus came to fulfill the Law. What does "fulfill" mean? We generally understand that it means to accomplish, to carry out by his words and actions the Old Testament prophesies about him, as we see here in Matthew:

> "This was to fulfill what was spoken through the prophet Isaiah:
>
> > 'Here is my servant whom I have chosen,
> >   the one I love, in whom I delight;
> > I will put my Spirit on him,
> >   and he will proclaim justice to the nations.
> > He will not quarrel or cry out;
> >   no one will hear his voice in the streets.
> > A bruised reed he will not break,
> >   and a smoldering wick he will not snuff
> >   out,
> > till he leads justice to victory.
> >   In his name the nations will put their
> >   hope.'"
> (Matthew 12:17–21)

Jesus was the fulfillment of the above passage from Isaiah 42:1–4. There are at least fifteen other such passages in Matthew alone that refer specifically to the fulfillment of Old Testament prophesies (1:22; 2:6, 15, 17, 23; 4:14; 5:17; 8:17; 12:17; 13:14, 35; 21:4; 26:54, 56; 27:9).

But it goes beyond this—Jesus not only fulfilled specific prophesies, he fulfilled the whole Old Testament by living it out perfectly. And even further, in him is embodied the fulfillment of all that was spoken about the Kingdom.

The second understanding that we note is that the reference to "the Law and the Prophets" refers to the whole Old Testament. The Jews divided the Old Testament into three sections: the Law or Torah, the Prophets and the Writings. But they commonly referred to the entirety of the Old Testament by mentioning only the first two: the Law and the Prophets.

The third understanding has to do with the reference to "iota" and "dot." The iota is the smallest Greek letter. "Dot" is generally taken to refer to *keraia,* which is the smallest stroke of the pen in written Hebrew.

Problem with Pharisaic Legalism

Putting all this in the context of Jesus' message and ministry, these words are very significant. Jesus was affirming the validity and authority of the Old Testament Scriptures. Jesus did not have a problem with the Old Testament; his problem was with the legalistic system that the scribes (teachers of the law) and Pharisees had manufactured around the Law, with their focus on externals and on details instead of on people and heart.

We don't think we can beat this drum too much. As we strive to put into practice Jesus' words, we have to be very careful not to fall into the trap of the Pharisees. It is so much easier to deal with externals and details than with people and heart, and probably less messy. Eugene Peterson's paraphrase of verses 17-18 in *The Message* is clarifying:

> "Don't suppose for a minute that I have come to demolish the Scriptures—either God's Law or the Prophets. I'm not here to demolish but to complete. I am going to put it all together, pull it all together in a vast panorama. God's Law is more real and lasting than the stars in the sky and the ground at your feet. Long after stars burn out and earth wears out, God's Law will be alive and working."

Obeying Jesus' Teaching

Moving on to verse 19, we read:

> "Anyone who breaks one of the least of these commandments and teaches others to do the same will be called least in the kingdom of heaven, but whoever practices and teaches these commands will be called great in the kingdom of heaven."

What is so striking about this passage is the grace that

undergirds it. We can seriously mess up and still be "in the Kingdom." What Jesus says here is shocking really. We can fail to live perfectly and we can even teach someone wrong doctrine, but we can still be in the Kingdom—least in the Kingdom, but still in the Kingdom. This is hard to grasp, but I am so thankful for a gracious God.

Jesus goes on to tell us that greatness in the Kingdom is based on simply doing and teaching God's will—it is not about pedigree; it is not about politics; it has nothing to do with public opinion. The Gallop Poll is not the Lamb's book of Life!

Again, let's hear from Peterson's paraphrase:

> "Trivialize even the smallest item in God's Law and you will only have trivialized yourself. But take it seriously, show the way for others, and you will find honor in the Kingdom."

All that is fine and good, but it is verse 20 that really gives us the most difficulty—and also the most insight:

> "For I tell you that unless your righteousness surpasses that of the Pharisees and the teachers of the law, you will certainly not enter the kingdom of heaven."

Keep in mind what was said earlier about the fourth beatitude. "Righteous" does not mean "religious" nor does it have anything to do with "legalistic observance." Jesus focuses here on maximum attitude, not minimum requirements.

Remember the story of the rich young ruler? It seems like much of the modern world that we live in is preoccupied with the same thing that he was: a concern with the absolute minimum requirements for salvation. What do I "have to do" to be saved? The Pharisees' answer to that question was: "more"—more than the law required. And they went on to define very specifically what that meant, often "building a fence around the law"—that is adding more laws that would keep you from breaking the original law.

Jesus' approach was completely different, which we will see over and over as we continue to study the Sermon. Jesus was like them in moving us away from "minimalist" thinking, but unlike them in putting the emphasis on the heart not outward requirements.

Not New-and-Better Legalism

One of the dangers of studying the Sermon on the Mount that we have talked about repeatedly is developing a new and better legalistic system—"to out-Pharisee the Pharisees," so to speak. One person we know sincerely asked, "Does exceeding the righteousness of the teachers of the law and Pharisees mean that since they fasted twice a week (Luke 18:12) then I need to fast three times a week?" Some of us tend to find this kind of thinking comforting and safe. "Just tell me what I have to do, and I will do it." That is *not* what Jesus is talking about.

To help us understand this concept, let's look at how this passage fits into the Sermon. It introduces a series of six references to the Old Testament and juxtapositions the Pharisees' understanding of them with the kingdom understanding that Jesus came to bring.

1. Verses 21–26: Do not murder (Exodus 20:13, Deuteronomy 5:17).
2. Verses 27–30: Do not commit adultery (Exodus 20:14).
3. Verses 31–32: Whoever divorces his wife let him give her a certificate of divorce (Deuteronomy 24:1).
4. Verses 33–37: Do not swear falsely, but perform to the Lord what you have sworn (Leviticus 19:12, Deuteronomy 23:21–23).
5. Verses 38–42: Eye for an eye and tooth for a tooth (Exodus 21:24, Leviticus 24:20, Deuteronomy 19:21).
6. Verses 43–48: Love your neighbor (Leviticus 19:18) but hate your enemy.

Jesus stresses the importance of "heart," of caring about people and not just the abstract following of the law. Looking for legal loopholes was a favorite practice of the scribes and Pharisees (see Matthew 15:1–20). Trying to find some way around the commands, some way to excuse our behavior is totally foreign to Jesus' thinking. When our heart is to please our Heavenly Father and to love our brother, then the "command" is not a "burden" at all.

As we have talked with people in various churches about these kingdom concepts, we have realized how deeply ingrained some of this "scribes and Pharisees legalism" is in our faith family. Many who struggle with a wrong emphasis on trying to be "perfect" have found it extremely freeing to see Jesus' focus here, both on the grace of the above verses as well as the emphasis on heart and attitude that we find in this text.

We also see in these passages that Jesus considers his word just as authoritative as the Old Testament law. The people who were listening got this point, as we see in the postscript to the Sermon in Matthew 7:28–29:

> When Jesus had finished saying these things, the crowds were amazed at his teaching, because he taught as one who had authority, and not as their teachers of the law.

Exceeding the Righteousness of the Pharisees

Our text could also be said to set up the rest of the Sermon, as Jesus shows exactly what he means by "exceeding" the righteousness of the scribes and Pharisees throughout the remainder of his message. After discussing the six examples mentioned above, he goes on to talk about giving, praying and fasting, then covers materialism and judging before wrapping up with a discussion of false prophets and putting the Sermon into practice. In all of this he is contrasting his take on things with the views of the scribes and Pharisees, but beyond that he is showing us the essence of age-to-come living in this present age.

The construction here in Greek for "you will never" is a

double negative, a no-no in English but absolutely fine in Greek.[1] The NIV translates it "certainly not" and the Holman and ESV both use "never." Strong language at any rate. If our earlier comments are correct, you can mess up pretty badly, and yet, Jesus is not preaching a cheap grace. He is saying that if your righteousness does not exceed or surpass that of the scribes and Pharisees, you won't even make it in the door—*no never!*

In looking at the fourth beatitude we have already seen how closely connected the idea of righteousness is to right relationships. We have seen how this starts with our relationship with God and spills over into every relationship we have.

Notice how the statement in 7:12 fits in with this idea of the central role of relationships:

> "So in everything, do to others what you would have them do to you, for this sums up the Law and the Prophets." (Matthew 7:12)

Jesus here says that treating others as we want to be treated sums up the teaching of the entire Old Testament! This idea is borne out in other passages such as Matthew 22:37–40:

> Jesus replied: "'Love the Lord your God with all your heart and with all your soul and with all your mind.' This is the first and greatest commandment. And the second is like it: 'Love your neighbor as yourself.' All the Law and the Prophets hang on these two commandments."

And then we have Paul's words in Galatians 5:14 as well:

> The entire law is summed up in a single command: "Love your neighbor as yourself."

I (Steve) was sharing this with a brother who was struggling with feeling like he could never measure up; so since he was doomed to fail, why even try? Have you ever felt like that? He was encouraged by Jesus' words here as he began to see that God views righteousness in terms of relationship rather than as "measuring stick" religion in which you can never measure up and had no chance of success.

I am not saying we can ever live this out perfectly. If we are ever tempted to think we can, then we have to go back to beatitude number one all over again.

True Righteousness

So in summary, perhaps the difference in the righteousness of the Pharisees and the true righteousness of the Kingdom can be seen in this diagram (see figure 3).

God wants us to focus first on him and then as a result on all the others around us. Righteousness is all about *heart*, about caring, about loving God and the people around us. All of them!

Pharisee Righteousness	Kingdom Righteousness
From self	From God
For self	For God
Outward	Inward then outward
Not really righteousness	About right relationships

Figure 3

But to keep from getting overwhelmed, focus on one relationship to start with. What does it mean to be righteous in this relationship? What can I do to be righteous in this relationship this week?

Questions for Study and Discussion

1. How could we misunderstand what Jesus said about our righteousness exceeding that of the scribes and Pharisees?
2. So what does it mean for our righteousness to exceed that of the scribes and Pharisees?
3. In what ways might we be tempted to adopt a new and better legalism? How would that be at odds with the Beatitudes?
4. In what ways do you want to seek God's righteousness?

12
Kingdom Relationships

"You have heard that it was said to the people long ago, 'Do not murder, and anyone who murders will be subject to judgment.' But I tell you that anyone who is angry with his brother will be subject to judgment. Again, anyone who says to his brother, 'Raca,' is answerable to the Sanhedrin. But anyone who says, 'You fool!' will be in danger of the fire of hell."

Matthew 5:21–22

G iven what we have looked at in the previous chapter concerning righteousness, it is not surprising that Jesus now begins to address how relationships will be handled by kingdom people. In this passage we have the first of six occasions when Jesus refers to what people have heard in the past contrasted with what Jesus is calling for in the Kingdom.

As we begin to look at these specific situations, perhaps it is good to be reminded of something we said in the previous chapter. We must be on our guard against legalism. There is a tendency for people to read the Sermon and come away with responses such as these:

- "He didn't say anything about...so there is no rule."
- "He said, 'If someone sues you.' He didn't say we couldn't sue someone else."
- "He says, 'Don't judge,' so you shouldn't be giving me correction."
- "He says lust is like adultery in the heart, so I have grounds to divorce my husband."

Such comments could be multiplied, but they all have one thing in common: They are grounded in legalistic thinking, and here is the problem with that.

- The Beatitudes are the foundation for everything in the Sermon, and everything about the Beatitudes moves away from legalism and moves to matters of the heart.
- Everything concerning Jesus' statement about the Pharisees and their idea of righteousness moves away from legalism.
- There is a difference in emphasizing obedience and promoting legalism. Jesus calls for obedience to the deeper principles, but he hates straining out gnats and swallowing camels (Matthew 23:24).

- Legalism is basically self-focused, with the person either seeking to justify himself, have his own way, or find a way to exalt himself. Obedience is concerned with pleasing God and demonstrating trust in him, his character and his way.

Our concern, then, must not be to hear a new rule or law, but to find the deeper principle that reflects God's will. In the Sermon, Jesus addresses a number of specifics, but there are a whole host of issues that he does not address. It would be a mistake to think that in regard to these matters Jesus has nothing to say. The principles we find in the issues he does address can be applied to many other areas. There is a tenor of life here that we need to grasp.

Over the Top

If you watch for it, we think you will see that Jesus is continually beckoning us to what we might call an "over the top" type of righteous response that goes beyond anything that law might require. By the time we get to the sixth and final contrast, Jesus will actually use a word that almost means the same thing as our phrase "over the top." And he will make it clear that this is the normal expectation for kingdom living.

This over-and-beyond quality is a vital part of the kingdom ethos. When the age to come breaks into the present age, the people who embrace it will have a different character and will respond in ways that are often dramatically different.

There will be nothing minimalist about their approach.

Of course, the people had long heard, "Do not murder." But now they hear Jesus say, "Anyone who is angry with his brother will be subject to judgment." The phrase "with his brother" is probably most significant. It is appropriate to be angry about wrongdoing, but the problem comes when anger becomes personal and is directed against the individual and not just against the condition.

Jesus goes on to say that we should not speak of other people with words of contempt (in this example, "Raca"— a Syriac term of derision). Likewise, we should not put others down, saying such things as "you fool." The Greek word for fool is *moros* from which we get the English word "moron."

We find this particularly interesting in view of something recently posted on a website by one who openly declares himself a Christian on his financial talk show. A listener wrote to him asking that he stop calling the credit card company that the listener works for a "bunch of morons."

The talk show host replied: "I don't owe an apology at all. I've dealt with your company for years, and I have a track record of dealing with enough of you to know that 'morons and idiots' *absolutely applies*, so I do not owe you an apology—not even close." He seems to have missed Jesus' clear teaching as well as the larger principle.

Jesus is telling us that "Do not murder" is just a beginning point when it comes to how we treat people. We may speak out against wrongdoing, but turning our verbal wrath on another person or group of persons is not the kingdom way. It would be helpful for us to see that in all Jesus' examples and teaching in Matthew 5 what the law says is never an ending point but just the place to start. The kingdom person will go far beyond this point.

Leave Your Gift

We see this principle of "going beyond" in the next statement Jesus makes.

> "Therefore, if you are offering your gift at the altar and there remember that your brother has something against you, leave your gift there in front of the altar. First go and be reconciled to your brother; then come and offer your gift.
>
> "Settle matters quickly with your adversary who is taking you to court. Do it while you are still with him on the way, or he may hand you over to the judge, and the judge may hand you over to the officer, and you may be thrown into prison. I tell you the truth, you will not get out until you have paid the last penny." (Matthew 5:23–26)

To appreciate how the first-century Jew would have heard these words, we need to understand something about the temple and the way in which the ritual sacrifices were offered. In figure 4 on the next page we have a diagram of the temple area. The average Jew who was coming to offer a sacrifice had to go through quite a series of steps. He would first come into the Court of the Gentiles where he

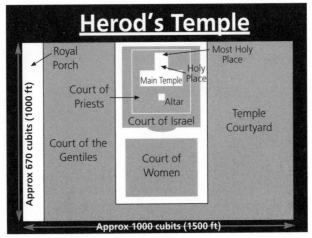

Figure 4—www.ebibleteacher.com

would either get the animal that he had brought for sacrifice approved by one of the priests, or he would purchase an animal that was already approved. The animals could only be purchased with the local currency, and if he had come from some distance, he likely would have to deal first with the moneychangers.

Once he had his approved sacrifice, he would make his way through the Court of the Women and into the Court of Israel. He would then take his place among the other worshipers and wait for the priests to go through their ritual, which included offering a large sacrifice on the altar. Following this, the priests would allow the men to approach the altar with their sacrifices.

So with this background, Jesus says that if you get all of this done and it is almost your time to offer your gift, but then and there you remember that your brother has something against you, you should put down your gift and go out through the Court of the Women, out through the Court of the Gentiles and out to wherever you find your brother and seek to be reconciled with him. Then, you can come back and with a pure heart and clear conscience offer your sacrifice to God.

Is Jesus giving us a law here, or is he laying down a great principle of kingdom living? Isn't he saying, "Don't stop with not murdering. Go all the way to recognizing that working out reconciliation with your brother is crucial in your relationship with God"? Surely, he is teaching us to take extraordinary measures, if that is what is required, to deal with the hurt that our brother may feel or with some matter that has broken our relationship.

The Center of the Target

Here we have a biblical principle that the two of us have written extensively about in our book *One Another*.[1] From a kingdom perspective, relationships are at the center of the target, never somewhere on the periphery. Peace, harmony and unity are essential characteristics of the kingdom life, and whenever any of these is damaged, getting things right is of the highest priority.

As we maintained in Volume One, we desperately need each other in order to live as kingdom people. Relationships are part of the warp and woof of the Kingdom. At the same time our relationships express the reality of the Kingdom as we show it to the world together. And, thank God, they give us support, as well as correction, to keep receiving the Kingdom.

In view of this teaching, it is quite amazing how many people are able to compartmentalize their relationship with God and see it as having little or nothing to do with their relationships with other people. Jesus would appear to have his own "compartment" for such people, and it is not to be found in his Kingdom.

"Settle matters quickly" should be a dictum that we all live by. Personal issues that are not resolved will only fester and lead to more serious problems. Settling matters or resolving conflicts is something that many of us dread. Even if we have had experiences that were painful, we must develop an environment in which we all realize that attention should be given quickly when there are strained or broken relationships or anything less than unity.

So, starting with the command that we have heard to not murder, Jesus takes us far beyond to the pursuit of real fellowship and harmony. In this first example, Jesus clearly raises the bar, and in the remainder of Matthew 5 we will see him do it again and again. We will be challenged to take it higher.

Questions for Study and Discussion

1. What would you say is the difference between emphasizing obedience and emphasizing legalism?
2. In the statements about being angry at people and demeaning them with pejorative terms, what is Jesus teaching us about relationships?
3. Describe all that one had to do to offer his sacrifice in the temple. Then using as much detail as possible, describe what Jesus said to do if you at that moment remember your brother has something against you.
4. What is the deeper principle here, and why is reconciliation so important?
5. How do you see this applying to relationships in your life that may not be good?

13
Kingdom Purity

"You have heard that it was said, 'Do not commit adultery.' But I tell you that anyone who looks at a woman lustfully has already committed adultery with her in his heart. If your right eye causes you to sin, gouge it out and throw it away. It is better for you to lose one part of your body than for your whole body to be thrown into hell. And if your right hand causes you to sin, cut it off and throw it away. It is better for you to lose one part of your body than for your whole body to go into hell."

Matthew 5:27–30

In July 2007 psychologist Albert Ellis died at age ninety-three in New York City. In 1982 he was ranked second to Carl Yung and ahead of Sigmund Freud by his peers as the most influential man in his field. He was the originator of Rational Emotive Behavior Therapy. Available on the Internet is his article "Fifty Reasons That Masturbation Is Good for You." Earlier he had commented on this passage from Matthew with these words: "If Jesus wanted to make rules against adultery for his religious followers, that was his right, but he was entirely wrong to prohibit what a person should think."

As we have talked about kingdom living, we have seen it is usually the opposite of the world's idea about living. Nowhere do we see this more clearly illustrated than with this passage and this famous thinker's response to it.

You would have to live under a rock to miss the fact that we live in a world that relishes and celebrates and certainly makes money off of something that Jesus says we must not have in our hearts. From American preoccupation with the *Sports Illustrated Swimsuit Edition* to the $100 billion dollar worldwide porn industry, material designed to encourage lust is pervasive.

To many people it seems that lust is victimless sin. Nobody gets hurt so why be concerned? We should be more worried about child abuse and drunk driving and saving the environment; lust is not really hurting anyone. It is widely accepted as just part of life. It is one of the sins that is joked about countless times a day. But do we forget that outward sinful actions always begin in the heart and the mind?

A recent study found that 20% of U.S. government workers spend time at work viewing Internet pornography. Surveys taken in *conservative* churches consistently find that more than 50% of the men admit to having viewed pornography in the previous month. Of course that says nothing about where the minds of people, both men and women, are 24/7. You don't have to be a *Sports Illustrated* reader or be on the Internet to do what Jesus is talking about here. All it takes is to open your eyes and let a little imagination take you where it wants you to go.

God's Gift

Jesus doesn't specifically say here that sex is God's gift, but this is a biblical teaching, and it is surely the reason why he says what he does about the misuse of this gift. Jesus taught, as do the Scriptures as a whole, that sexuality is good. God created it and intends it to be expressed in a special way in the marriage relationship. We will talk about this topic more when we move on to the next passage.

Americans are familiar with the message of the ASPCA (American Society for the Prevention of Cruelty to Animals). Animals are valuable and important and should not be mistreated or abused. The world says "Yes, yes." What Jesus is saying here is that sexuality (which is so intrinsic to our humanness) is valuable and special and is not to be abused or misused. Most everyone agrees with this to some extent. Every society has their norms and rules in regard to sexuality.

But who should set the boundaries, us or God? Who best knows how God's good gift is to be used? Do we leave it to the ever-changing field of psychology to tell us what is rational, ethical and healthy? No, kingdom living is all about reestablishing our covenant with our Creator and putting ourselves under his rule and reign. It is about trusting him with everything.

A Matter of Heart

Life in the Kingdom of God is always about the heart and not just outward actions. You see this all the way through the Sermon. As God told Samuel in an Old Testament context, "Man looks at the outward appearance, but the Lord looks at the heart" (1 Samuel 16:7).

Jesus would later say this in Matthew 15:19:

> "For out of the heart come evil thoughts, murder, adultery, sexual immorality, theft, false testimony, slander."

The world thinks that what is going on in the heart is a person's own business. But God is in the business of changing men's hearts. For that to happen we have to give God all our hearts, not just some compartments. This is what all the examples in the Sermon are about: not just externals, but changing our hearts.

Let's just think about several examples.

- Suppose a man is wealthy and generous and uses his wealth to help people get an education and housing, but in his heart he never deals with his racism? How does God view such a man?
- Or suppose a person is evangelistic and is successful at bringing lots of people to hear the good news, but in his heart he is still arrogant and prideful? How does God view such a person?
- Suppose a man volunteers and serves in the body of Christ, but continues a pattern of indulging his lust?

How does God view such a person?

- Suppose he provides for his family, spends time with kids, remembers all his wife's important dates, but spends hours viewing pornography? How would his wife view her husband? How would God view his faithfulness?

The word "lust" comes from the Greek *epithymeō*, a word or a form of it that is used many times in New Testament. The root meaning is "desire" and is overwhelmingly used to mean self-centered desire—particularly the desire to have or possess. Noticing that someone is attractive is not lust, but desiring to have what is attractive and to use it for one's pleasure is where lust begins.

Jesus says lust is "committing adultery in your heart." What does unfaithfulness do to your heart? Does it draw you to God? How much does lust inspire you to show mercy? How much does it help you to listen and care? How eager are you to share the good news after indulging your lust? What effect is it having on your character?

About Relationships

Everything Jesus is talking about has to do with relationships. And in this case it is all about how we view, treat and use or refuse to use another person made in the image of God. A little bit later on in the Sermon, Jesus tells us that we should treat others the way we want to be treated. What Jesus is talking about here is not treating people as objects for our gratification but rather treating them with respect.

It is very important for us to realize that the opposite of hate is not "not hating" but love. The opposite of anger is not "not being angry" but kindness. The opposite of lust is not "not lusting" but caring about others. Lust is about self-gratification. Caring is about meeting the needs of others

Purity is much more than *not* doing something. Maybe you hear the question in the fellowship: "Brother, how is your purity?" He answers: "Good. I haven't been involved in any lustful things in months." But what have you been involved in? A pure heart is not an empty heart. It is not just a heart where there is no lust. It is a heart where there is love and giving and caring.

Radical Response

As Jesus keeps speaking, he takes us deeper, showing even more the dramatic contrast between the world and the Kingdom of God. If we tell someone in the world that we have this problem with lust, what is the reaction? "So what? Enjoy it. Don't feel guilty. That is normal. That is what people do." Jesus takes a very different approach.

> "If your right eye causes you to sin, gouge it out and throw it away. It is better for you to lose one part of your body than for your whole body to be thrown into hell. And if your right hand causes you to sin, cut it off and throw it away. It is better for you to lose one part of your body than for your whole body to go into hell." (Matthew 5:29–30)

Sometimes we are asked if we take the Bible literally. The right answer is, "No, not all the time." Because it employs figures of speech, it is not meant to be taken literally. However, we should always take the Bible seriously.

The way Jesus sets this up lets us know that it is figurative and hyperbole. There would not be a time when your right eye would cause you to sin but your left eye would not. So what is Jesus' point? Do whatever you need to do to deal with the sin in your heart. And if this means taking some radical steps, so be it. Our good friend, Gordon Ferguson, shared this formula with us:

- Evaluate (all the time, or at least very regularly)
- Regulate (when your evaluation shows that you are not practicing self-control)
- Amputate (when the regulation isn't working)

So how does this play out? We all know what comes into our homes over the TV can be bad, so we *evaluate* what is happening and understand how it is tempting us. If we see that some things are not good, then we need to *regulate.* For example, watch only with another person, or only with your wife, or don't sit up late watching TV alone. If that is not working and you are breaking your rules, then *amputate.* In other words, get rid of the TV. Wait! You mean…get rid of it? Yes. Do whatever it takes, remember?

But watch out for language that can be deceptive. We have a tendency to talk about how "I slipped into sin" or how "I fell into sin." Our friend David Mundie, one of the elders in Nashville, offers a needed corrective. He says: "It is not that we fell. We walked right in, consciously opening door after door that our consciences put up to stop us, and by the time we are on the computer or doing something else, we have already made several deliberate choices to ignore the Spirit who was screaming in our head."

Jesus' teaching is impossible for the natural man. You may be thinking, "Let me out of here! These people are nuts! Nobody can do this." You are absolutely right. It is only possible by the grace of God and with the power of the Spirit. The person who lives this kingdom message will be praying, "Have mercy on me, Lord Jesus," or some other earnest prayer more times than he can count. We will be brought back to the first beatitude many times. As Jesus makes clear in the Lord's Prayer that we will look at in Matthew 6, we will not be sinless. We will be in need of ongoing forgiveness, but we can be freed from the slavery of sin, in this case our lust.

It is a constant battle to keep our hearts pure, loving and focused on caring for others and to not use them to gratify our desires. It takes a daily conscious dependence on God.

Life to the Full

However, Jesus is teaching that we can live full lives without lust. Do we hear him? Do we believe him? He is saying we can. He is not saying it is easy. Nothing he says in this Sermon on kingdom living is easy because we are living out heaven's values on earth. But he is saying we can do it.

To find purity in our world is amazing because it is such the exception. It is powerful because it seems so impossible. But we hear about amazing things all the time. A blind man climbs Mount Everest; a student-athlete with no legs wins a collegiate wrestling championship; a teenage girl sails solo around the world; a mother without arms has children and cares for them with her feet, and a man swims 139 miles in the open sea without stopping.

We could go on. Most impossible things don't get done because people don't believe they can be done. Jesus believes that when the Kingdom breaks into this world, sexual purity is possible.

Questions for Study and Discussion

1. Respond to this comment: "With all the big problems in the world, why would we want to spend time talking about lust? It is just something that is a part of our humanness."
2. Why is God so concerned about what is happening in our hearts?
3. How does lusting affect our ability to live out other kingdom qualities?
4. Talk about how the call to "evaluate, regulate, amputate" would be applied to your life.

14
Kingdom Marriage

"It has been said, 'Anyone who divorces his wife must give her a certificate of divorce.' But I tell you that anyone who divorces his wife, except for marital unfaithfulness, causes her to become an adulteress, and anyone who marries the divorced woman commits adultery."

Matthew 5:31–32

The next section is short and not very sweet—just direct and to the point. It could be tied in to the former paragraph that deals with purity; in some translations it is combined.

You will remember that Jesus gives six illustrations of Old Testament quotes and contrasts the contemporary take on them by the Pharisees with his response: "but I say." This is one of the six but the introductory formula varies. Five of these begin with some form of "you have heard that it was said" while this one starts with "it was also said" indicating that it is very closely tied to the previous idea.

David Scaer puts this passage in a "Kingdom coming" context and offers a valuable insight.[1]

> The situation of the original paradise in Genesis is being reconstituted in Jesus, who has appeared as the new Adam. The relationship between a husband and wife will follow the prototype of man, not in his fallen condition, but in his pristine state where the male and female constituted one flesh or person. Genesis 1 and 2 is normative, not Genesis 3. A community tolerating divorce seemed to be an open denial of that community's purpose as God's new creation.

Examining the teaching of marriage, we may want to return to our idea in the previous chapter that the opposite of lusting is not "not lusting." Purity is by nature a *positive* thing, not just the absence of bad. In the same way, the opposite of divorce is not just staying married but being faithful in marriage.

This is reminiscent of the story Jesus told in Matthew 12:43–45:

> "When an evil spirit comes out of a man, it goes through arid places seeking rest and does not find it. Then it says, 'I will return to the house I left.' When it arrives, it finds the house unoccupied, swept clean and put in order. Then it goes and takes with it seven other spirits more wicked than itself,

and they go in and live there. And the final condition of that man is worse than the first. That is how
it will be with this wicked generation." (Matthew
12:43–45)

Our focus here, and we believe Jesus' focus, is not so
much on forbidding divorce as elevating marriage. The goal
is much more than not getting a divorce. The goal is faithfulness to our spouse as we live out the Beatitudes in our
marriage. To use language that will later come from Paul to
husbands: loving as Christ loved the church.

All of this ties back in to what we have been talking
about every step of the way on this kingdom journey: embracing the reign of God in our lives and living out his will
here on earth. In heaven there are no broken commitments,
only faithfulness.

Shut the Back Door

There is some difficult language here that we may not
completely understand, such as the following: "anyone who
divorces his wife, except for marital unfaithfulness, causes
her to become an adulteress." To fully comprehend it we
most likely need to understand more about the Jewish culture in which women were clearly in the disadvantaged position. But the overall message for kingdom-first people
surely cannot be missed: "When you get married, close the
back door and stay faithful and stay married."

It is a dramatic and scandalous fact that divorce rates in
evangelical churches are often higher than in general culture.

A recent study by the Barna Research Group revealed that divorce rates among conservative Christians were significantly higher than among other faith groups, and much higher than among atheists and agnostics. That telling statistic shows how little interest most "believers" have in Jesus' call to live heaven on earth.

To get a more complete view of what Jesus thought about this subject, we have to go to Matthew 19:3–9:

> Some Pharisees came to him to test him. They asked, "Is it lawful for a man to divorce his wife for any and every reason?"
>
> "Haven't you read," he replied, "that at the beginning the Creator 'made them male and female,' and said, 'For this reason a man will leave his father and mother and be united to his wife, and the two will become one flesh'? So they are no longer two, but one. Therefore what God has joined together, let man not separate."
>
> "Why then," they asked, "did Moses command that a man give his wife a certificate of divorce and send her away?"
>
> Jesus replied, "Moses permitted you to divorce your wives because your hearts were hard. But it was not this way from the beginning. I tell you that anyone who divorces his wife, except for marital unfaithfulness, and marries another woman commits adultery."

It helps to know some of the Jewish rabbis' teaching about this subject during the first century. The Mishnah, which was the first collection of the rabbinical teachings, was assembled about AD 200 but reflects some of the discussion about divorce that was going on in rabbinical circles in Jesus' day. Consider these quotes found in the Mishnah.

Gittin 9.5

The School of Shammai says,
A man may not divorce his wife unless he has found unchastity in her, for it is written, Because *he hath found in her indecency in anything* (Deut 24:1).

And the School of Hillel says,
[He may divorce her] even if she spoiled a dish for him, for it is written, *Because he hath found in her indecency in anything* (Deut 24:1).

Rabbi Akiba says,
Even if he found another fairer than she, for it is written, *And it shall be if she find no favour in his eyes* (Deut 24:1).

Rabbi Shammai was a contemporary of Jesus. Rabbi Hillel probably died before Jesus began his ministry (his grandson was Gamaliel, whom we encounter in the book of Acts). Rabbi Akiba lived in the late first century. Jesus' teaching reinforces that of Rabbi Shammai, which for obvious reasons, was not the most popular view. But how did Jesus' disciples feel about his teaching here? "The disciples said to him, 'If such is the case of a man with his wife, it is better not to marry'" (Matthew 19:10). In a word: They were shocked. But he wasn't finished…

Jesus replied,

> "Not everyone can accept this word, but only those to whom it has been given. For some are eunuchs because they were born that way; others were made that way by men; and others have renounced marriage because of the kingdom of heaven. The one who can accept this should accept it." (Matthew 19:11–12)

The Bottom Line

What can we learn from these teachings?

Marriage is for life. One man, one woman for life! "Until death do us part" is not just flowery language. Our attitude should be to invest in our marriages. This is the only way to keep marriage growing for a lifetime. What better way to spend money and/or time than going on a marriage retreat or a get-away weekend with your spouse, taking a marriage course, or getting people involved to help you in your marriage. That is kingdom-first thinking! Marriage is a God-given chance to grow.

Sex is powerful. Sex outside of marriage is the only thing that God allows to "break" the marriage bond because it violates the one-flesh principle. The allure of an affair is powerful. Sexual temptation in various forms plagues many of us from puberty on. But sex is something profound and has a powerful effect on those involved in it. This passage in 1 Corinthians 6 helps us understand how significant it is:

> Do you not know that he who unites himself with a prostitute is one with her in body? For it is said, "The two will become one flesh." (1 Corinthians 6:16)

Even when one intends for sex to be merely casual or recreational, Scripture—with amazing psychological insight—teaches that something with deep implications is happening there.

Divorce is devastating. In the well-known text in Malachi 2:16 God actually says that he "hates" it. Let's look at the context and consider why God feels so strongly about divorce.

> Have we not all one Father? Did not one God create us? Why do we profane the covenant of our fathers by breaking faith with one another?
> Judah has broken faith. A detestable thing has been committed in Israel and in Jerusalem: Judah has desecrated the sanctuary the LORD loves, by marrying the daughter of a foreign god. As for the man who does this, whoever he may be, may the LORD cut him off from the tents of Jacob—even though he brings offerings to the LORD Almighty.
> Another thing you do: You flood the LORD's altar with tears. You weep and wail because he no longer pays attention to your offerings or accepts them with pleasure from your hands. You ask, "Why?" It is because the LORD is acting as the witness between

> you and the wife of your youth, because you have broken faith with her, though she is your partner, the wife of your marriage covenant.
>
> Has not the LORD made them one? In flesh and spirit they are his. And why one? Because he was seeking godly offspring. So guard yourself in your spirit, and do not break faith with the wife of your youth.
>
> "I hate divorce," says the LORD God of Israel, "and I hate a man's covering himself with violence as well as with his garment," says the LORD Almighty.
>
> So guard yourself in your spirit, and do not break faith. (vv10–16)

Once again we see the concern for faithfulness in relationships that we talked about in chapter 11. God hates it when we break faith, when will fail to be true to the commitments we have made to other people.

But you as a reader may wonder just how much we know about divorce. I (Steve) would have to say, personally, not much. I have been married thirty-five years, and actually in both of our families there is only one divorce and that was one of my cousins. So I guess we know something about staying married. Diane's aunt and uncle celebrated seventy-five years of marriage, and they have three children who have all been married more than fifty years. Such a pattern has to start somewhere, and in my case it was with my grandparents' three kids, ten grandchildren, fifteen great grandchildren and only one divorce. That is not the norm in our day, but it can start and it can start with you.

Of course, our very human family did not escape every type of dysfunction, but we have been spared the devastating effects of divorce. We must decide that as kingdom people, divorce is not an option to be entertained except in that most egregious of circumstances that Jesus describes, and even then it is not required.

Just recently we were able to talk with an evangelist and wife from another city. He was married as a disciple right out of college, but his wife was unfaithful to him and eventually left him. Graciously God gave him a great wife and family and ministry, but he still struggled deeply with feeling like God had cursed him. He eventually went through six months of therapy to be able to cope with these feelings. Divorce, the failure of the marriage, is devastating.

Marriage is not for everyone. We have not heard much in our faith family about this teaching of Jesus that some are better off not marrying. This is not because they are strange or weird or somehow deficient, but because of the Kingdom. Paul thought the same way, as we see in 1 Corinthians 7:26–35. Both Jesus and Paul taught it. We must study and teach it. Marriage is sacred, but there is something greater: one's relationship with God. Marriage is sacred, but you do not have to be married to share in the sacred.

In some situations our teaching has gone in the other direction, with an emphasis on the idea that everybody should be married. The bottom line of such teaching is that people then feeling like they should get married unless there is something "wrong" with them. This is unbiblical thinking. We need to get on the same page with Jesus and Paul. Marriage is not for everyone, and some people will be better able to serve God and serve others by remaining single. We need to honor and hold up these brothers and sisters.

Even today, just like in the New Testament times, there are dangerous and difficult places that the gospel needs to go and that would be best served by men and women who are only committed to Jesus and not concerned about a spouse and family.

Practical matters. How does the church apply the teaching on marriage (which many consider brutally difficult) in our contemporary situation? We would offer these observations.

1. This passage in combination with the one in Matthew 19, the similar but differing passages in Mark 10 and Luke 16, and Paul's words in 1 Corinthians 7, present difficult hermeneutical or interpretive challenges. On this particular subject entire books have been written. The scope of this book does not allow an extensive examination of all the perspectives.

2. People do become disciples of Jesus and enter the Kingdom of God after many violations of God's original plan of one-man, one-woman for one life. Two or more marriages along with various types of blended families bring about situations and complicated connections not easy to untangle. The exact

shape of repentance will be a matter of judgment and must be sought with the greatest of humility.

3. However, since entering the Kingdom does constitute a new creation, we must trust that God has taken away the old and has given the person who is born anew a fresh start. No new Christian can retrace all his steps, undo all his wrongs and make everything right. He counts on the grace of God for a new birth to a new life.

4. But then we come to another "however." Once we have become disciples, we realize we are committed to God's original plan for mankind before the Fall, so that breaking the one-flesh relationship through divorce and remarriage is not an option for us.

5. Christians will still sin and depart from God's plan after baptism, but they must hold up God's high standard, even if it means a level of self-denial and kingdom-first thinking that many may think should not be expected. One's desire for marriage (or specifically, another marriage) must never be put before one's surrender to God.

Conclusion. Marriage is a solemn commitment. The world says, "You can always get a divorce if it doesn't work out," or "You have a right to a happy marriage," or "You have the right to leave an unhappy one." The world's thinking must be totally rejected by Christians. What we must say is, "I am as committed to this marriage as I am committed to God."

The really hard times in marriage can teach us the most valuable lessons. Does it sometimes seem God allows people to suffer too much in their physical health? Yes. What advice would we give people in that situation? Does it look like God allows people to suffer too much in their marriages? Yes. Shouldn't we apply that same thinking to this kind of suffering as well?

So often people look for a reason why divorce would be okay ("so I can be about the pursuit of my happiness") instead of committing to stay in a marriage and live out the Beatitudes and message of the cross.

Absolutely none of this makes any sense to those not seeking first the Kingdom of God. So let us seek first the Kingdom.

"Father, may your Kingdom come to each of our hearts and lives. May your will be done in us, in our lives, in our marriages, just like it is in heaven. In the name of Jesus, your Son. Amen."

Questions for Study and Discussion

1. Why should we expect faithful covenant keeping in marriage to be a part of the kingdom life?
2. How do we need to think about faithfulness and unfaithfulness in marriage?
3. How can we hold to Jesus' high standard for marriage and still deal with the complicated dilemmas people are in because of having ignored God's standard? Where does God's standard for forgiveness fit in?
4. Why is it so important for every married disciple to "close the back door"? How can we expect God to work in such a decision?

15

Kingdom Honesty

"Again, you have heard that it was said to the people long ago, 'Do not break your oath, but keep the oaths you have made to the Lord.' But I tell you, Do not swear at all: either by heaven, for it is God's throne; or by the earth, for it is his footstool; or by Jerusalem, for it is the city of the Great King. And do not swear by your head, for you cannot make even one hair white or black. Simply let your 'Yes' be 'Yes,' and your 'No,' 'No'; anything beyond this comes from the evil one."

Matthew 5:33–37

This brings us to the fourth of the "you have heard it said" passages. And once again we must emphasize that we are looking at how to live the way of heaven on earth. These are not arbitrary rules; they are the description of the kingdom heart.

We want to see here the same emphasis on a positive attitude that we saw in the earlier text, rather than just an emphasis on eliminating the negative behavior. Just as the teaching on lust was not solely about not lusting, but on caring for one another, this passage is not just about not taking oaths, but it is about being people who tell the truth.

In our world, truth telling seems in short supply. "Spin" seems to be the operative word. Crafting a sound bite that conceals the truth is a skill that is highly sought after. When one of the most famous phrases of our time, spoken by one who was at the time the leader of the free world, is "it depends on what the meaning of the word 'is' is," you know just about everything you need to know about our efforts to avoid truth telling.

We hear politicians strongly denounce charges against them. There are athletes who fiercely deny using performance-enhancing drugs. We have large corporations that go to extremes to hide their actions and their motives. But in almost every case ultimately the truth comes out, and we see that a combination of lying and deception was the mode of operation.

The Secretary of Defense was testifying before the U.S. Congress as we were doing final edits on this book. An angry senator asked him, "Why are we doing business with countries that lie to us?" The straight-talking secretary didn't hesitate for a moment and replied, "Most countries lie, Senator. That is the way business gets done" (Robert Gates, appearing before a Senate panel, June 15, 2011).

We gain a better understanding of the context into which Jesus is speaking when we look at his words later in Matthew 23:16–22 where he points out how the lawyers and teachers sought to evade or manipulate the truth:

> "Woe to you, blind guides! You say, 'If anyone swears by the temple, it means nothing; but if anyone swears by the gold of the temple, he is bound by his oath.'
>
> "You blind fools! Which is greater: the gold, or the temple that makes the gold sacred?
>
> "You also say, 'If anyone swears by the altar, it means nothing; but if anyone swears by the gift on it, he is bound by his oath.' You blind men! Which is greater: the gift, or the altar that makes the gift sacred?
>
> "Therefore, he who swears by the altar swears by it and by everything on it. And he who swears by the temple swears by it and by the one who dwells in it. And he who swears by heaven swears by God's throne and by the one who sits on it."

We can see the complicated system they developed. The heart of the legalists was to keep the letter of the law but always to look for ways to get around the law, which included ways to get around telling the truth.

Jesus cuts through all of this rigmarole in Matthew 5:37 by saying, "Let your 'Yes' be 'Yes' and your 'No,' 'No.'" In other words just tell the truth all the time, and if you do, you will be believed and won't have to swear to convince anyone.

Oaths

Though it is clear that the principle here is to always tell the truth, we are most sympathetic toward the view that says we should not ignore Jesus' specific teaching on oaths either. To be true to Jesus' teaching shouldn't we not only tell the truth all the time, but also emphasize the truth by refusing to take oaths? Because the laws of the United States are based on some biblical principles, the U.S. court system has always recognized the convictions of some that oaths are contrary to God's law, and so in court you are always allowed to affirm rather than swear that you will tell the truth.

Because of this passage, it makes sense to us that we should affirm rather than swear. If this view of oaths should seem legalistic, we would argue that the same thing might have been said in Jesus' day, but he goes out of his way to say that kingdom people will take an entirely different tack. It makes sense to us that such strong statements of conviction in our day give us an opportunity to call attention to the vital importance of transparency and truth telling. Jesus' statement that anything more than your simple "yes" or "no" comes from the evil one is a poignant statement not to be overlooked.

Importance of Truth Telling

But now let us consider three ways that truth telling is crucial to kingdom living.

1. Lying and deceit show no confidence in God's sovereignty or in his work for good in the lives of his people. We lie, we conceal the truth, and we avoid transparency because we do not believe that God can use the truth. We believe that our lives will somehow be better if the truth is not known. Basically, we lie or tell half-truths because we do not trust God. We are trying to manipulate the situation according to our agenda instead of allowing God to work in the reality of the facts. No wonder we have passages like this one found in Proverbs 6:

> There are six things the LORD hates,
> seven that are detestable to him:
>> haughty eyes,
>> a lying tongue,
>> hands that shed innocent blood,
>> a heart that devises wicked schemes,
>> feet that are quick to rush into evil,
>> a false witness who pours out lies
>> and a man who stirs up dissension among
>>> brothers. (vv16–19)

Of the seven things that are detestable to God, two of them are lying. All our efforts to avoid truth telling are our efforts to play God and refuse to acknowledge his sovereignty and kingship.

Generally there are three reasons why we lie:

- To avoid getting in trouble.
- To make ourselves look better, thus feeding either our pride or our insecurity.
- To get something we want by manipulating others.

When we place ourselves under God's reign, we give up all of our tricks of the trade and lessons learned on the street, and we trust that his grace and power are sufficient to strengthen and bless us as we live our lives in full disclosure.

2. Dishonesty, lying and a lack of truth telling destroys relationships. It should be crystal clear by this point that kingdom living is all about relationships—building them, maintaining them and growing them in healthy ways. But is there anything that destroys relationships faster than a lack of honesty?

When we find that someone has lied to us, we feel the painful violation of the relationship. We hurt; we feel angry; we may feel like a fool; but most of all, we lose trust in the person who has lied to us. Many marriages have been damaged more by the lying than the action that was lied about. And the same could be said for many types of relationships.

The lack of truthfulness comes into our relationships in many ways. We could be deceitful by just letting someone believe something that is not true when it is to our advantage. Certainly the wisdom of the world will tell you to use this tactic as often as possible.

Of course, a large part of the honesty and integrity Jesus is addressing here has to do with following through with what you say you will do. So, if you borrow money, then repay it. If you say you will come and help someone, then show up and help. If you say you will call someone back, then make the call. When we fail to follow through with our commitments, we certainly hurt our relationships; and if our actions are seen to be hypocritical, then we are often casting a bad reflection on God himself in the minds of some people.

If we are weak in this area, then we need to get help and make decisions to repent. We need to go to those we have disappointed and confess it, asking for their forgiveness. Then we need to show fruits of repentance. We must not ever underestimate how vital truth telling, honesty and integrity are in the kingdom life.

3. The great cosmic battle between good and evil, between God's Kingdom and the kingdom of this world, could be defined as the battle between truth and lies. This idea seems to find support in a host of biblical texts:

- John 8:31–32—To the Jews who had believed him, Jesus said, "If you hold to my teaching, you are really my disciples. Then you will know the truth, and the truth will set you free."
- In John 18:37–38—Jesus said to Pilate, "You are right in saying I am a king. In fact, for this reason I was born, and for this I came into the world, to testify to the truth. Everyone on the side of truth listens to me." "What is truth?" Pilate asks.
- Romans 1:25—They exchanged the truth of God for a lie, and worshiped and served created things rather than the Creator.
- Romans 2:7–8—To those who by persistence in doing good seek glory, honor and immortality, he will give eternal life. But for those who are self-seeking and who reject the truth and follow evil, there will be wrath and anger.
- 1 Corinthians 13: 6—Love does not delight in evil but rejoices with the truth.

- Ephesians 5:8–9—For you were once darkness, but now you are light in the Lord. Live as children of light (for the fruit of the light consists in all goodness, righteousness and truth).
- 1 John 1:6–10—If we claim to have fellowship with him yet walk in the darkness, we lie and do not live by the truth. But if we walk in the light, as he is in the light, we have fellowship with one another, and the blood of Jesus, his Son, purifies us from all sin. If we claim to be without sin, we deceive ourselves and the truth is not in us. If we confess our sins, he is faithful and just and will forgive us our sins and purify us from all unrighteousness. If we claim we have not sinned, we make him out to be a liar and his word has no place in our lives.

When we think about what goes on around us each day, which do we find more prevalent, truth or lies? Again, from our friend David Mundie comes this observation that seems to sum up so much of the posture of our culture: "There are websites out there that let you download essays and term papers. A quick survey reveals that every one of them that I checked on has a paper on the theme of 'honesty.' So in the world you can take an essay on honesty and put your name on it and turn it in to your teacher, thus lying about your paper on honesty."

When it comes to politics, most of us would agree that democracy is a better form of government than dictatorship or tyranny. But even in a democracy, it almost seems that the whole system for choosing leaders is based on who tells the most believable lies, though we know both sides are lying.

In the perfect Garden that God created, sin was introduced with a single lie. After Eve correctly told Satan what

God had told them—that they would die if they ate the fruit of a certain tree—this is what Satan says in Genesis 3:4–5:

> "You will not surely die," the serpent said to the woman. "For God knows that when you eat of it your eyes will be opened, and you will be like God, knowing good and evil."

Satan has been promoting this same lie ever since. He convinces us that if we sin, we will not die but that somehow we will know more and be gods ourselves. The truth is that God is the source of all human life, so if we separate ourselves from him, we are guaranteed to die.

Are we tempted to lie to our spouses, to lie about money or what we were doing on the Internet? Are we tempted to lie to our children about why we can't spend time with them? Teens, are you tempted to lie about where you went or who you went with? Students, are you tempted to lie to your teacher about why your homework is late or who did your homework or if you got help on a take-home test? Are we tempted to lie to our bosses about the status of the project we are working on? Are we tempted to lie to a client to keep our boss happy? Are we tempted to lie on our tax forms, or our mortgage or job applications? When we do lie, do we justify it, or do we confess it?

Confessing lies seems to be twice as hard as confessing other sins because we are often confessing the first sin *and the lie* at the same time. When we confess though, we are showing God that we trust him to forgive us.

Here on earth we are in the cosmic battle that requires us to choose between good and evil. The leader of one side is our God, who cannot lie and whose power is unlimited. On the other side is Satan, who is called the father of lies and whose natural language is lies and whose power is limited and who knows he has already lost. His biggest lies, which he started in the Garden of Eden, continue today to profess that there is no battle at all or that if there is, it really does not matter.

We have to choose whether we stand for truth or for lies. When we lie, we have chosen to stand with Satan in the battle at that moment; but when we are truthful, we are standing with God and showing ourselves to be citizens of heaven.

Questions for Study and Discussion

1. Why should we not be surprised to find teaching on honesty in a sermon on kingdom righteousness, which has everything to do with kingdom relationships?
2. How does it affect you when you know someone has lied to you or shaded the truth?
3. When are you most tempted to lie or tell a half-truth?
4. What character traits do we show when we live our lives with transparency?

16
Kingdom Nonresistance

"You have heard that it was said, 'Eye for eye, and tooth for tooth.' But I tell you, Do not resist an evil person. If someone strikes you on the right cheek, turn to him the other also. And if someone wants to sue you and take your tunic, let him have your cloak as well. If someone forces you to go one mile, go with him two miles. Give to the one who asks you, and do not turn away from the one who wants to borrow from you."

Matthew 5:38–42

We come now to what is usually considered the most controversial section of the Sermon. Four times Jesus has referred to the Old Testament, and four times he has raised the bar by saying "but I say to you," and then giving his call for something much higher. Now he makes a fifth statement about what had been taught under the old covenant, and this time seemingly goes off the charts, or in some people's minds, off the tracks.

We have observed that Jesus' kingdom teaching is in every way opposite to the "wisdom of this world." This is never more true than it is here with this passage and with the one that will follow about loving our enemies. Many people, on hearing these words, are ready to stand up and shout, "This makes no sense." But let us remember what we have said earlier: These are the words of Jesus, and he does expect us to put them into practice.

Don't Resist

Let's start with the original Old Testament concept of "eye for eye, and tooth for tooth." Though this may have a harsh sound to it, it was a restrictive measure. First of all, this was not something an individual could put into practice on his own. It had to be part of a judicial procedure. If your enemy does some damage to you, the law of revenge and the impulse of human nature is to do something back to that person and then add a little bit for good measure to teach them a lesson. This law meant that the revenge or punishment would have to be limited to doing something only equally severe to the original perpetrator.

However, once again Jesus raises the bar and this time raises it extraordinarily high: "Don't resist an evil person." We once asked a large audience of longtime believers how

many of them had ever heard a sermon or teaching on this
subject. One lone hand was raised. If there is any teaching
in the Sermon that we almost universally avoid, it is this one.
And yet, this is so ironic because what Jesus says here is at
the heart of his own Passion. His death for our sakes would
not have taken place had he not had conviction about this
and lived what he taught. We find it interesting that we can
appreciate something Jesus did for us, but not want to have
any part of doing it ourselves. Is this not the posture of the
majority of religious people?

It is our belief that with this passage we are at a most
crucial point in our study of the Sermon. Certainly our hearts
have already been challenged and tested, but now they will
be really tested. The writer of Hebrews quotes from the
Psalms, using the same verse three times within a short span
of sentences. The passage says, "Today if you hear his voice,
do not harden your hearts." As we hear the voice of Jesus in
this text, it is most important that we not harden our hearts.
How we handle these words of Jesus will go a long way in
determining whether or not we really live the kingdom life.
In this section we are seeing the revolutionary teaching that
it is not God's plan to overcome evil with evil, for that does
not reveal the Kingdom. No, evil must be overcome by good.

"Do not resist an evil person." We must all ask ourselves,
"How will I obey this teaching? How will I put it into practice? As a disciple-maker, how will I teach others to obey
this that Jesus commands?" These are questions we must not
avoid or evade. We must not put them in the file marked

"Things I Don't Understand." You may decide not to teach or practice what we as the authors of this book will teach, but you must decide, if you're going to follow Jesus, what you will teach.

Consider this: You read Jesus' words and let your mind run quickly and imagine a home invasion where an intruder is threatening your family. You then say, "Of course, I would resist that person and protect my family." Then you let that comment be a decisive response that shuts down your thinking and keeps you from wrestling with this text. It is our experience that this is fairly common, and yet, it is no way to handle the words of Jesus. If you need to stop and pray at this point before going on, that would be a very appropriate and kingdom way of doing things.

Important Observations

Before we get into some of the examples Jesus gives, let us make four preliminary observations.

First, the context here, with the Old Testament reference, is a situation of revenge or retribution. The import of Jesus' message is that we should get rid of all desire for revenge. Getting even should not even be a consideration.

Second, the examples that he gives will be showing us that the kingdom life calls us to an "over the top," even creative, righteous response in all areas of our lives. There is no hint here of what a friend of ours calls "minimalistic legalism."

Third, we need to hold in our minds the truth that God's way of getting things done is often very different from man's way. We must remember that Peter was convinced that Jesus going to the cross was the wrong thing—so much so that he took him aside to rebuke him for such a thought. We must be careful not to make the same mistake.

Fourth, embedded in all these responses is the concept of Jesus' followers denying themselves and taking up the cross. If we are asserting ourselves and fiercely holding onto our rights, nothing he teaches here will be possible for us.

Several Examples

In the first example Jesus says, "If someone strikes you on the right cheek, turn to him the other also." Since most people are right handed, striking someone on the right cheek would naturally involve striking them with the back of the hand. In Jewish society this meant a great insult. So Jesus would seem to be teaching that if we are insulted, not to retaliate, but to also go beyond that and offer the other cheek. In so doing, we show the perpetrator that we are not controlled by his evil but have a freedom to respond in a most unexpected way.

In the second example, Jesus says, "If someone sues you and wants to take your tunic, give him your cloak as well." The tunic was a long shirt that the people wore against the skin and most people had more than one. The cloak was the heavier outer garment, somewhat akin to an overcoat that many people also used as a blanket at night. It was against Jewish law to sue someone and take his cloak. Jesus is seriously teaching a most uncharacteristic response to a lawsuit. The natural mind wants to quickly go on the defense. Jesus calls for a revolutionary generosity that again would probably be rather shocking, and even convicting, to the plaintiff.

Is Jesus not teaching us to take a whole new approach to lawsuits? Is it not amazing how many disciples of Jesus today will quickly initiate a lawsuit just as long as they legalistically follow the principle that the person they are suing is not a brother? Do we not consider that how we interact with him might lead him to become a brother?

In his third example Jesus says, "If someone forces you to go with him one mile, then go with him two." Soldiers in the occupying Roman army could require the people to carry their gear for one mile, and there were mile markers along the main roads much as we have on our interstate highways. Of course, the Jews despised this requirement and considered it degrading. But again, Jesus' kingdom teaching is to "go beyond" and to "go over the top," showing that the disciple is not controlled by resentment but is free to serve. Would you suppose that this response was intriguing to the Roman soldiers?

Jesus' fourth example is to "give to the one who wants to borrow from you." This one does not seem to be exactly parallel to the other three, unless we suppose that the one who wants to borrow from you is a "good for nothing" fellow who is just trying to take advantage of you. Even if that were the situation, Jesus encourages us to have a heart to give.

Should we give money to the fellow on the street corner who likely will use it to buy booze or drugs? We would advise against it. There is also the Jesus principle of being wise as serpents and harmless as doves. And yet, there is a generosity being taught here that we must embrace.

As we were finishing the last edits on this book, I (Tom) spoke with a Christian friend I saw as we both were leaving a local restaurant. When I remarked to her that it was unusual to see someone leaving breakfast with such a large box of leftover food, I discovered that it was an extra meal she had bought for the homeless man she had observed selling papers on the corner when she came in. I was convicted and want that kind of heart.

How Do We Respond?

Somewhat surprisingly, we have found that when these principles are taught, even longtime disciples react as if they were just punched in the stomach. They feel there's been an assault on their rights, their dignity, their instinctive sense of self-preservation. Although these statements are a part of Jesus' most famous sermon and appear in the earliest stages of the New Testament, it is as though many are reading them for the first time.

Obviously Jesus' words bring up fear in us—fear of being run over, being dominated, looking weak, losing our dignity. We must ask if those feelings are prompted by the Spirit or by our flesh. But let us suppose we don't do what Jesus tells us to do. Will we strike the evil person back or even kill in self-defense? Will we fight the lawsuit or even sue others ourselves? Will we resent it when we are compelled to do something degrading and decide to do just the minimum, and that with an attitude? Will we refuse the one in need who wants to borrow from us? Can we see ourselves doing any of these things with the spirit of the Beatitudes?

Teaching and Practice of the Early Church

What did Christians in the early centuries teach on this subject? How did they understand Jesus?

- Athenagoras (c. AD 175, E 2.129)—We have learned not to return blow for blow nor to go to law with those who plunder and rob us. Not only that but to those who strike us one side of the face we learned to offer the other side also.
- Tertullian (c. AD 200, 3.712)—If someone attempts to provoke you by physical violence, the admonition of the Lord is at hand. He says, "To him who strikes you on the face, turn the other cheek also." Let their outrageousness be worn out with your patience.
- Tertullian Apology (c. AD 197—VVV)—[Although] Christians were sufficiently numerous to offer successful resistance to persecuting emperors, did they not count it better to be slain than to slay?
- Cyprian (c. AD 250, 5.462)—When a Christian is arrested, he does not resist. Nor does he avenge himself against your unrighteous violence—even though our people are numerous and plentiful.

- Lactantius (c. AD 304; 313, 7.160)—The Christian does injury to no one. He does not desire the property of others. In fact, he does not even defend his own property if it is taken from him by violence. For he knows how to patiently bear an injury inflicted upon him.

The teaching of Jesus and this practice of it by the early Christians goes so much against human nature. Why in the world would they have chosen to live this way, except that they pledged allegiance to Jesus as their Lord and King?

Questions Raised

There are two important questions that are often raised by this teaching.

First, is this "doing nothing"? We would say the answer is clearly, "No." It is doing something; it is loving. In the face of insult, injury or requirements, the disciple is free to think about the other person and to want him or her to see the Kingdom. It is not doing nothing; it is trusting God. This is precisely Peter's point regarding Jesus in 1 Peter 2:

> When they hurled their insults at him, he did not re-taliate; when he suffered, he made no threats. In-stead, he entrusted himself to him who judges justly. He himself bore our sins in his body on the tree, so that we might die to sins and live for right-eousness; by his wounds you have been healed. (vv23–24)

In not defending his rights, in not endorsing Peter's action with the sword, in not calling down twelve legions of angels, Jesus was being conscious of God (1 Peter 2:19) and "entrusting himself to him who judges justly."

Second, will this really work? The answer of course depends on what we mean by "does it work?" No, not if we mean we will never be harmed and everything will always turn out well. But the answer is "yes" if we mean this action will show the world the distinctiveness of the Kingdom. At the same time we might be surprised at how often a creative, uncharacteristic response to a threat may produce a result that would be far better than drawing a gun or grabbing a knife.

We frequently hear advertisements for courses on self-defense indicating that people understand the importance of making preparation for unexpected attacks or intrusions. But because Christians have often not taken seriously Jesus' words, we have likely done very little to prepare ourselves to give uncharacteristic and creative responses to those kinds of events. What would happen if we began such preparation by at least envisioning possible intrusions of evil, and then used our imagination to conceive of uncharacteristic non-violent and selfless responses? What would happen if we prayed consistently to be able to respond in these ways?

Some of us may have seen on television or the Internet the story of a man who recently came into an office, pointed a gun at the woman there and demanded the money that he expected to find in this loan company. The woman fell on her knees and began to pray for the assailant. Eventually he put the gun down and began to share his painful life story with the woman. Since we have been looking for such stories, this is just one of many that we have heard about. How do we know what God would do in such situations if we only gave him a chance?

At the end of a recent sermon on this topic I (Tom) shared some thoughts, convictions and decisions that I have made:

1. I do not find this easy, and I cannot answer every hypothetical question.
2. I need much help from God and my brothers and sisters to live this message.
3. I have made a decision to practice a lifestyle of revolutionary nonresistance.
4. I have made a decision not to retaliate or to harm another person physically or emotionally under any circumstance.
5. I have made a decision to pray and to prepare my mind for those unexpected times when my conviction would be put to the test.
6. I've made the decision to share the good news of the Kingdom with anyone who tries to harm me or take something from me.
7. I have made the decision to seek an atypical creative response if I am sued.
8. I have made the decision not to sue others.

9. I have made the decision to seek to overcome evil with good.
10. I have made the decision to continually confess to God my own inability to live this way without his help and to ask for the power of the Spirit.

Remarkably, this principle from Jesus is on the same page in most of our Bibles as his command to reconcile relationships, to be faithful in marriage and not to lust. Surely we must want to be as devoted to this one as we are to the others. If this calls for more radically trusting God than we have before, let it be. These responses to evil are a most powerful way to show the world that the Kingdom is breaking into this present age.

Questions for Study and Discussion

1. Having just studied honesty, share your honest gut-level response to Jesus' teaching on nonresistance.
2. Would you say the church has taught on this topic as much as on other topics, such as lust, that we find in Matthew 5? If not, why do you suspect that is true?
3. What are you responses to the decisions that Tom said he has made?

17

Kingdom Love for Enemies

"You have heard that it was said, 'Love your neighbor and hate your enemy.' But I tell you: Love your enemies and pray for those who persecute you, that you may be sons of your Father in heaven. He causes his sun to rise on the evil and the good, and sends rain on the righteous and the unrighteous. If you love those who love you, what reward will you get? Are not even the tax collectors doing that? And if you greet only your brothers, what are you doing more than others? Do not even pagans do that? Be perfect, therefore, as your heavenly Father is perfect."

Matthew 5:43–48

For the first time in the Sermon on the Mount (and in the New Testament for that matter) we hear Jesus speak the word "love." How interesting that his first command for us to love found in the Gospels is the command to love our enemies. What the people had heard was "love your neighbor and hate your enemy." This statement was never made in the Old Testament, but one can understand why it would have become a common thought. For one thing, David is found expressing hatred for his enemies often in the Psalms.

Jesus raises the bar as high as it will go in preaching this radical ethic of love: "Love your enemies." Don't hate them; don't be bitter toward them; don't seek revenge; don't hope they will have bad fortune; and don't want to remove them from your sight. No, instead care about them; want them to be blessed, and take action to show goodwill toward them. If we have not realized it already, we certainly see in this command the need for supernatural help to live the kingdom life.

Clear Teaching

In order to consider all the aspects of this teaching it will be helpful to see the parallel verses in Luke 6 and Paul's words in Romans 12 (see figure 5 on the next page).

Before you read any further, we suggest you look at these three texts and write down the specific and clear teachings that you see. Once you've done that, come back and continue your reading to see if you have found the same ones we have. We believe it is vitally important for every disciple to develop his or her own convictions about these words of Jesus, and we believe this exercise will help you do that.

Matthew 5:43–48	Luke 6:27–36	Romans 12:17–21
"You have heard that it was said, 'Love your neighbor and hate your enemy.' But I tell you: Love your enemies and pray for those who persecute you, that you may be sons of your Father in heaven. He causes his sun to rise on the evil and the good, and sends rain on the righteous and the unrighteous. If you love those who love you, what reward will you get? Are not even the tax collectors doing that? And if you greet only your brothers, what are you doing more than others? Do not even pagans do that? Be perfect, therefore, as your heavenly Father is perfect."	"But I tell you who hear me: Love your enemies, do good to those who hate you, bless those who curse you, pray for those who mistreat you... "Do to others as you would have them do to you... "But love your enemies, do good to them, and lend to them without expecting to get anything back. Then your reward will be great, and you will be sons of the Most High, because he is kind to the ungrateful and wicked. "Be merciful, just as your Father is merciful."	Do not repay anyone evil for evil. Be careful to do what is right in the eyes of everybody. If it is possible, as far as it depends on you, live at peace with everyone. Do not take revenge, my friends, but leave room for God's wrath, for it is written: "It is mine to avenge; I will repay," says the Lord. On the contrary: "If your enemy is hungry, feed him; if he is thirsty, give him something to drink. In doing this, you will heap burning coals on his head." Do not be overcome by evil, but overcome evil with good.

Figure 5

Now that you have looked at all three passages, take your list and compare it with ours.

1. Love your enemies.
2. Pray for those who persecute you.
3. Don't love just your brothers. To do that is to be like everybody else.

4. Loving like this is loving like God.
5. Have an indiscriminate or perfect love like God has.
6. Do good to those who hate you.
7. Bless those who curse you.
8. Pray for those who mistreat you.
9. Do to your enemies as you would want them to do to you.
10. Do good to your enemies.
11. Lend to them without expecting to get anything back.
12. Do not repay anyone evil for evil.
13. Do not take revenge.
14. If your enemy is hungry, feed him.
15. If your enemy is thirsty, give him something to drink.
16. Do not be overcome by evil, but overcome evil with good.

This is an impressive list, and we must conclude that Jesus' teaching on the subject, which was passed on to Paul, is in no way vague or unclear. The kingdom person is not commanded to feel great affection for his enemy, but he is commanded to treat him with concern and goodwill and to do so in very specific ways.

Our experience in teaching this at different times and in different places tells us that it is important for you to stop again at this point and write down all the thoughts, feelings and questions that these statements bring up in you. Once you've done that, come back and finish the chapter.

Processing Jesus' Teaching

Now that you are beginning to process this arguably most radical of Jesus' teaching, let us tell you some of the actual responses that we have heard from ministry leaders who have studied this text with us:

- What does this mean?
- Am I even a disciple/Christian?
- Who then can be saved?
- This is challenging.
- Who is my enemy?
- Was this just about persecution situations?
- What about military service?
- I naturally think "what does this not mean?" but I know this is not the place to go first.
- I am reminded that only a few will be saved. To do this I will have to get prepared and be deliberate.
- Not killing my enemy is only the beginning of loving my enemy.
- This is the message of the cross.
- This challenges me down to the core.
- Jesus gives a high calling. We can't be looking for the minimum but must go to the maximum.

Were any of the responses you wrote down similar to these? Without a doubt these words of Jesus stir up our thinking. Some of us have been disciples of his for a long time and have never really come to grips with these matters. It is time that we did so.

Raising the Bar

We want to diagram the places Jesus has taken us here in Matthew 5 and look "graph style" at how he keeps raising the bar. We are called to higher ground in the Kingdom because Jesus believes that with the help of God we can go much higher.

Take a moment to consider each of these graphs (figures 6-11).

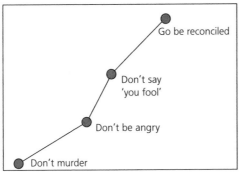

Figure 6

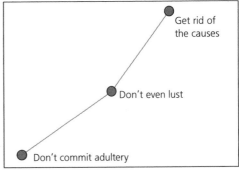

Figure 7

Figure 8

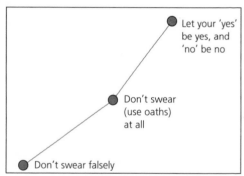

Figure 9

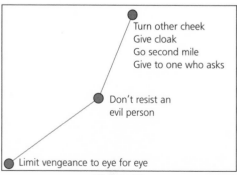

Figure 10

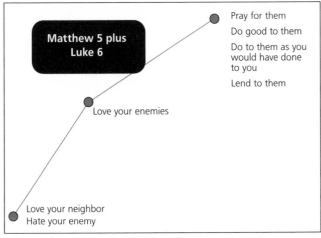

Figure 11

At every point Jesus begins with the common understanding of what would be the right thing to do, and then
he raises the bar higher and higher. If we have followed the
trajectory pattern of his points, we are not surprised to see
how he calls us to treat our enemy.

Dietrich Bonhoeffer's comments on this passage seem
particularly insightful and poignant, and we will quote from
him extensively. He describes this passage as the most crucial point in the Sermon, and gives this reason:

> Here, for the first time in the Sermon on the Mount, we
> meet the word which sums up the whole of its message,
> the word "love." Love is defined in uncompromising terms
> as the love of our enemies. Had Jesus only told us to love
> our brethren, we might have misunderstood what he

meant by love, but now he leaves us no doubt whatever
as to its meaning.[1]

We have had people tell us that they don't know how
this passage applies to them because they don't have any
enemies. Bonhoeffer points out that it was very different for
the disciples.

> The enemy was no mere abstraction for the disciples.
> They knew him only too well. They came across him
> every day. There were those who cursed them for under-
> mining the faith and transgressing the law. There were
> those who hated them for leaving all they had for Jesus'
> sake. There were those who insulted and derided them
> for their weakness and humility. There were those who
> persecuted them as prospective dangerous revolutionaries
> and sought to destroy them. Some of their enemies were
> numbered among the champions of the popular religion,
> who resented the exclusive claim of Jesus. These last en-
> joyed considerable power and reputation. And then there
> was the enemy which would immediately occur to every
> Jew, the political enemy in Rome.[2]

In this context then, Bonhoeffer finds that kingdom love
is truly defined.

> [The disciple's] behavior must be determined not by the
> way others treat him, but by the treatment he himself re-
> ceives from Jesus; it has only one source, and that is the
> will of Jesus. By our enemies Jesus means those that are
> quite intractable and utterly unresponsive to our love,

who forgive us nothing when we forgive them all, who respond to our love with hatred and to our service with derision.... Love asks nothing in return, but seeks those who need it. And who needs our love more than those who are consumed with hatred and are utterly devoid of love? Who, in other words, deserves our love more than our enemy? Where is love more glorified than where she dwells in the midst of her enemies?[3]

What Are You 'Doing More'?

Having said this, Bonhoeffer then carefully analyzes what he considers to be the most important verse in the passage: verse 47. His point can best be seen by looking at the English Standard Version: "And if you greet only your brothers, *what more* are you doing than others? Do not even the Gentiles do *the same*?" (emphasis added).

He calls attention to the phrase "what more are you doing than others?" "Doing more" translates the Greek word *perrison* which refers to that which is extraordinary; we might even say, as in a previous chapter, "over the top." He contrasts this with the expression "do the same" (*to auto* in Greek), and then he writes:

What makes the Christian different from other men is the "peculiar," the *perrison,* the "extraordinary," the "unusual," that which is not "a matter of course." This is the quality whereby the better righteousness exceeds the righteousness of the scribes and Pharisees. It is "the more," the "beyond all that." The natural is the *to auto* (one and the

> same) for heathen and Christian. The distinctive quality of
> the Christian life begins with the *perrison*.... The *perrison*
> never merges into the *to auto*. For [Jesus] the hallmark of
> the Christian is the "extraordinary." The Christian cannot
> live at the world level, because he must always remember
> the *perrison*."[4]

Bonhoeffer's emphasis on the word *perrison* seems entirely appropriate, as it is a word that plays a prominent role in the New Testament. Earlier when Jesus said, "For I tell you that unless your righteousness surpasses that of the Pharisees and the teachers of the law, you will certainly not enter the kingdom of heaven" (Matthew 5:20), he uses a form of the same word.

Consider some other meanings that are associated with this word: more, greater, excessive, abundant, exceedingly, beyond what is anticipated, exceeding expectation, more abundant, going past the expected limit, more than enough. Consider a diagram of the contrast (see figure 12).

to auto	perrison
the same, the normal, the usual	The extraordinary, the abundant, that which is over and beyond, exceeds expectations, is much greater

Figure 12

Perrison is used in other vital places in the New Testament to refer to the way God relates to us, as in these examples:

> "The thief comes only to steal and kill and destroy; I came that they may have life, and *have it abundantly*." (John 10:10 NASB, emphasis added)

> In him we have redemption through his blood, the forgiveness of sins, in accordance with the riches of God's grace that he *lavished* on us with all wisdom and understanding. (Ephesians 1:7–8, emphasis added)

And then we have this example of the Christians in Macedonia living the over-the-top life:

> And now, brothers, we want you to know about the grace that God has given the Macedonian churches. Out of the most severe trial, their overflowing joy and their extreme poverty *welled up* in rich generosity. For I testify that they gave as much as they were able, and even beyond their ability. (2 Corinthians 8:1–3, emphasis added).

Call to the Extraordinary

Bonhoeffer's point is as clear as it is right. In the Kingdom, Jesus calls us to the extraordinary, and he believes that because of the "much more of the Heavenly Father," which we will later discuss when we come to Matthew 7, we can live the "beyond all that." To fail to love our enemies and only love our brothers is to "do the same" that the heathen do. It would seem then that we who are disciples need to stop talking about how difficult and challenging this is and start embracing our new identity.

We need to trust that we can live by the power of the age to come and that doing the extraordinary, the amazing is quite expected.

Powerful Teaching

Today all of us need to be thankful for this truth and this teaching because without it we would not be in the Kingdom of God. Paul reminds us in Romans 5:10,

> For if, when we were God's enemies, we were reconciled to him through the death of his Son, how much more, having been reconciled, shall we be saved through his life.

For us to love our enemies is for us to do with others what God has done with us.

It is interesting to us that people will sometimes hear this teaching and ask, "Who is my enemy?" somewhat reminiscent of the man who asked Jesus, "Who is my neighbor?" It is almost as if they are thinking, "If someone is not my enemy, maybe I don't have to love him." But Jesus' message assumes that we will love our brothers and our neighbors and all those on the continuum even all the way out to our enemies (see figure 13).

Close Friends / Loved Ones···························Enemies

Figure 13

In Jesus' kingdom we will love all across the board. So there's no need to ask "Who is my neighbor?" or "Who is my enemy?" If they exist, we are to love them. This includes those who insult you, those who sue you, those who bully you, those who belong to a foreign force that occupies your country, those who defraud you, those who hate your country and want to destroy it, and those who want to blow you up, just to mention a few.

Bonhoeffer goes on to say:

> Christian love draws no distinction between one enemy and another, except that the more bitter the enemy's hatred, the greater his need for love. Be his enemy political or religious, he has nothing to expect from a follower of Jesus but unqualified love…. In such love there is no inner discord between private person and official capacity. In both, we are disciples of Christ, or we are not Christians at all.[5]

Public Life and Private Life?

The last part of the quote above is a repudiation of the classic argument formulated first by Augustine and then given great emphasis by Luther. It says that a Christian has a private life and a public life, and that these teachings of Jesus only apply to the conduct of the private life. In other words, when acting in some governmental role, Luther would say the Christian is not bound by this law of love. In such a case he is free to take off his citizenship in heaven and put on his citizenship in his country or his empire.

So here are the two views (figures 14 and 15):

The Christian is one undivided person—a citizen of the Kingdom all the time who lives by the principles of the Kingdom in all circumstances.	The Christian has a private life and a public life, and different rules apply. When he is in an official capacity he may do things he would not do just as a civilian.

Figure 14   **Figure 15**

The second position is the one held today by the great majority of people who describe themselves as Christians. It was a position unheard-of in the first 250 years of the church's life, but in the post-Constantinian era it has become dominant. Which one do you find more consistent with the teachings of Jesus?

Should a disciple act as a disciple all the time, or is he allowed to act in some other way if in a "public" role? Should he do good to his enemy in his "private" life, but even see a responsibility to harm his enemy in situations in his public life? If a disciple lives under the reign of God, are there times when he can legitimately say, "Jesus' words just do not apply to me in these circumstances"? In such a situation are we showing a higher allegiance to someone or something else than we are to Jesus?

Prayerful Consideration

Some of the possible implications of Jesus' teaching arouse very strong emotions in many people and often clash with deeply embedded cultural norms. We would urge you to prayerfully seek God's will, recognizing how powerful feelings and traditions can be, but affirming that our ultimate allegiance must be to God, his word and his often surprising ways of getting things done. This is always what it means to seek first his Kingdom and his righteousness—his righteousness that does *the extraordinary.* If we compromise Jesus' kingdom message at its most radical point, what kingdom will we be preaching, and what kingdom will we be in?

John Howard Yoder offered a carefully balanced but compelling insight when he spoke and wrote these words on more than one occasion:

> Christians love their enemies not because they think the enemies are wonderful people, nor because they believe that love is sure to conquer these enemies. They do not love their enemies because they fail to respect their native land or its rulers; nor because they are unconcerned for the safety of their neighbors; nor because another political or economic system may be favored. The Christian loves his or her enemies because God does, and God commands his followers to do so; that is the only reason, and that is enough.[6]

These comments seem most helpful particularly in situations where love for enemies can so easily be misunderstood. In the same spirit, we could add that the Christian does not love his enemies because he is unconcerned about the welfare of his family or because he does not recognize that some have resisted enemies with a spirit of self-less sacrifice. Again, he loves his enemies for the simple reason that this is what Jesus said people living the kingdom life will do.

Be Perfect?

It comes as no surprise then that this section ends with this verse: "Be perfect, therefore, as your heavenly Father is perfect" (v48). The call of the Kingdom is to imitate Jesus' love, and he was just living out what he learned from the Father. It is a high standard, but it is what Jesus calls us to. We should not understand "be perfect" as meaning without flaws or errors. Jesus is not demanding some kind of sinless perfection. He knows us all too well for that.

The word for "perfect" is *teleios,* which refers to completeness or maturity. But the meaning of Jesus' teaching is found more in the context. Both here in Matthew 5:45 and in the parallel in Luke 6:35, it is clear that we are to be like God in the way he is indiscriminate. We are to show as much love to our enemy as to our friend and as much love to the bad man as to the good one. The seriousness of our discipleship is revealed by how wholeheartedly we embrace Jesus' high call, which would seem to reach its pinnacle with this command.

Questions for Study and Discussion

1. How does the teaching in this chapter differ so drastically from that which is typically found in the world?
2. What is the effect when those claiming to be kingdom people don't wholeheartedly embrace Jesus' teaching about loving enemies?
3. What are your thoughts about this statement: "Our attitude toward our enemies is often shaped more by patriotism and nationalism than by the Scriptures, particularly Jesus' message"?
4. What is so crucial about the meaning of *perrison* and the idea of kingdom people doing the extraordinary?
5. Do you see a connection between this teaching and predictions about the Kingdom found in passages such as Isaiah 2:3–4 and Isaiah 11:6–9?
6. In what ways are you committed to loving your enemies?

18
Kingdom Rewards

"Be careful not to do your 'acts of righteousness' before men, to be seen by them. If you do, you will have no reward from your Father in heaven.

"So when you give to the needy, do not announce it with trumpets, as the hypocrites do in the synagogues and on the streets, to be honored by men. I tell you the truth, they have received their reward in full. But when you give to the needy, do not let your left hand know what your right hand is doing, so that your giving may be in secret. Then your Father, who sees what is done in secret, will reward you.

"And when you pray, do not be like the hypocrites, for they love to pray standing in the synagogues and on the street corners to be seen by men. I tell you the truth, they have received their reward in full. But when you pray, go into your room, close the door and pray to your Father, who is unseen.

> Then your Father, who sees what is done in secret, will reward you. And when you pray, do not keep on babbling like pagans, for they think they will be heard because of their many words. Do not be like them, for your Father knows what you need before you ask him." (Matthew 6:1–8)

Having raised the bar of true righteousness again and again, Jesus now turns his attention to the motivation for our actions. On the one hand, he has already taught us "Let your light shine before men" (Matthew 5: 16), but now comes the statement,

> "Be careful not to do your 'acts of righteousness' before men, to be seen by them. If you do, you will have no reward from your Father in heaven." (Matthew 6:1)

The purpose of the first (letting our light shine) is to glorify God. The purpose of the second is to bring glory to one's self, and Jesus takes dead aim at the latter.

The three subjects under discussion here—giving to the poor, prayer and fasting— were the foundational elements of Jewish piety and were often considered the most important works in the Jewish religion, as can be seen in this passage from Tobit 12:8:

Prayer and fasting are good, but better than either is almsgiving accompanied by righteousness...almsgiving delivers from death and purges away all sin.

Three Areas of Teaching

Perhaps in support of the priority of almsgiving, Jesus begins on that note and then addresses prayer and fasting, contrasting the negative with the positive—how not to do it with how to do it.

Giving to the Poor

It seems that some Jewish writers such as Tobit went so far as to see giving to the poor as a means of salvation. In contrast, the Greek and Roman culture as a whole did not encourage giving to the poor. Wealthy donors gave public contributions for public projects or to poor individuals in order to secure their popularity among the people, but normally not because of ethical or altruistic motivation.

Of course, what is being criticized in this passage is not the practice of almsgiving, prayer or fasting, but rather what one is seeking to accomplish while participating in these practices.

This verse is the introductory statement of the whole section. Jesus' point basically is that when you do your righteous deeds before others seeking their attention, then their praise is all the reward you're going to get.

William Barclay calls our attention to the fact that three times Jesus uses the phrase "they have received their reward" and that the Greek word *apechousin* for "reward" was the technical business and commercial word for receiving payment in full.[1]

> "So when you give to the needy, do not announce
> it with trumpets, as the hypocrites do in the syna-
> gogues and on the streets, to be honored by men.
> I tell you the truth, they have received their reward
> in full." (Matthew 6:2)

"Sound no trumpet" is surely the use of hyperbole or dramatic exaggeration, as we have no evidence that this was ever in actual practice. However, while there is no record that anyone ever used a trumpet to announce their offering, Jesus knew that people had their ways of making it known when they were giving their gifts.

This is the first time we find the word "hypocrite" in the New Testament. It does occur once in the Old Testament in Psalm 26.

> Test me, O LORD, and try me,
>   examine my heart and my mind;
> for your love is ever before me,
>   and I walk continually in your truth.
> I do not sit with deceitful men,
>   nor do I consort with hypocrites;
> I abhor the assembly of evildoers
>   and refuse to sit with the wicked.
> (Psalm 26:2–5)

Originally the word *hupokritai* was used to refer to someone who would come to a dinner and recite a long epic poem. It eventually was used to refer to an actor who was skilled at playing a role. By the time of the Septuagint, the translation of the Old Testament into Greek finished long before Jesus' time, the word was used in the sense of hypocrisy as we normally think of it: acting one way on the outside but being something else on the inside. Jesus uses the word fifteen times in the New Testament, with thirteen of those occurring in Matthew. Most of the time, the expression is in the plural.

As always, the context gives us plenty of clues to the meaning of the word. As we see in Psalm 26, it is parallel with the deceitful in the midst of a passage contrasting God's love and faithfulness with the wickedness of men. It clearly refers to those who play a role in life that seems spiritual and helpful when the heart is really focused on one's own self and gaining some kind of recognition. Jesus' message is for the kingdom person to consciously live without seeking to call attention to self:

> "But when you give to the needy, do not let your left hand know what your right hand is doing, so that your giving may be in secret. And your Father who sees in secret will reward you." (Matthew 6:3–4)

Again, we would take this as hyperbole. "Not letting your left hand know what your right is doing" is literally not possible, but Jesus is contrasting this with the hyperbole of blowing the trumpet. In one case action is taken to call attention to what "you" have done. Yet in the other, you don't even focus yourself on what "you" have done. The question is: Who are we trying to impress? Do we want the approval of men; do we want to be patted on the back or lifted up in front of others, or do we just want to please our Father?

Prayer

> "And when you pray, you must not be like the hypocrites. For they love to stand and pray in the synagogues and at the street corners, that they may be seen by others. Truly, I say to you, they have received their reward. But when you pray, go into your room and shut the door and pray to your Father who is in secret. And your Father who sees in secret will reward you." (Matthew 6:5–6)

Prayer, as we would expect, was held in high esteem by the Jews. Barclay tells us that one rabbinic saying was "He who prays within his house surrounds it with a wall that is stronger than iron." The rabbis lamented that it was not possible to pray every moment of the day. Rabbinic Judaism rightly saw prayer as an essential practice for the spiritual life, but for those who want to be given recognition, prayer can be used as an effort to impress.

We see the attitude of a hypocrite illustrated in Luke 18:11: The Pharisee "stood by himself" (ESV) to pray, suggesting that he was standing out in the middle of the courtyard in a very public way. Contrast that with the attitude of the tax collector who stood at a distance, or isolated himself from where the people were in order to pray to God.

In Matthew 6 we see the "do not pray like this," but "pray like that" pattern. The word "room" or "closet" as it was translated in the KJV or "inner chamber" as it is translated in the ASV, is from the Greek word that literally means

"storeroom" or "inner room." It conveys the idea of a room
in the house that had a door and thus afforded some degree
of privacy.

One thing we need to understand about our Father in
heaven is that he *sees*. As Hagar realized in Genesis 16:13,
the God who created heaven and earth is "the God who
sees." God is not unaware of what we are going through, of
our struggles, of our pain, of our suffering, of our joy, of all
that goes on in our lives. God sees.

> "And when you pray, do not keep on babbling like
> pagans, for they think they will be heard because of
> their many words. Do not be like them, for your Fa-
> ther knows what you need before you ask him."
> (Matthew 6:7–8)

The Jews had developed by this time standard prayers.
For example, the *Shema* was to be recited every day, along
with a series of short prayers called "The Eighteen." Though
we cannot be sure, it does not seem likely to us that Jesus is
referring to this practice, but to the tendency for some to pray
long prayers that seemed impressive.

When he says not to "keep on babbling like pagans," he
is referring to the prayers of the Gentiles, specifically the
Greeks, who when they prayed addressed the deity with as
many titles as possible, thinking that they could attract the
god's attention in that way.

It seems to be the way of men to think that the more and
the longer we pray the better. We, however, serve the

Almighty God who already knows what we need even before we ask him. It is not a matter of words; it is not a matter of length; prayer is primarily about relationship. Our Father wants to know us and wants us to know him. The truth is, this is the greatest reward: We get to know the Heavenly Father; we get to have a relationship with him.

The part of the Sermon in which Jesus teaches his disciples how to pray comes next in the text. This prayer (commonly referred to as the Lord's Prayer) merits the focus of an entire chapter, which will follow this one. So we move on to the third element, where Jesus addressed the subject of fasting.

Fasting

> "When you fast, do not look somber as the hypocrites do, for they disfigure their faces to show men they are fasting. I tell you the truth, they have received their reward in full. But when you fast, put oil on your head and wash your face, so that it will not be obvious to men that you are fasting, but only to your Father, who is unseen; and your Father, who sees what is done in secret, will reward you." (Matthew 6:16–18)

Interestingly enough, several of the commentaries that we consulted discuss both praying and giving to the poor at length, but failed to mention fasting at all. William Barclay mentions it but falls into the trap of so many.[2] He lists several reasons why fasting is good: for health, for self-discipline, to break habits, to learn to do without, to learn to appreciate your blessings. These are all true, but the biblical reason for fasting is none of these. It is simply to humble ourselves before God.

Jewish fasting also involved abstaining from certain other pleasures such as anointing your head with oil, which in the dry Mediterranean climate of the Middle East would be fairly obvious to those who saw you. Therefore Jesus teaches that anointing your head and washing your face were actually good things to do while fasting so that you don't call attention to the fact that you are fasting.

Of course, there is nothing negative here about the idea of fasting. The fact that Jesus says "when" you fast and not "if" you fast shows his support of the practice.

As is true throughout the Sermon, the emphasis in this section is on the heart and specifically here with our motivations. Why do we do the things we do? We have to get it clear in our heads that we can do the right things with the wrong motivation and for the wrong reason, and God will not reward us for it.

The key question: Are we serving the King or serving ourselves? Pleasing the King or pleasing self? If we live for the attention of others, that will be our full reward. If we live for the glory of God, we will receive his rewards and make an impact that will far exceed all we can imagine. However, there will be no thought that we deserve the first or should get credit for the second.

Questions for Study and Discussion

1. When do you find yourself most tempted to let others know the good that you have done?
2. How do you reconcile Jesus' teaching presented in this chapter with his call for us to let our light shine?
3. What do you understand Jesus to mean when he says, "They have received their reward"?
4. What reward do you get from serving with a desire to bring glory to God?
5. How do you keep your heart pure in this area?

19
The Kingdom Prayer

"Pray then like this:

"Our Father in heaven,
hallowed be your name.
Your kingdom come,
your will be done,
    on earth as it is in heaven.
Give us this day our daily bread,
and forgive us our debts,
    as we also have forgiven our debtors.
And lead us not into temptation,
    but deliver us from evil."
                                    Matthew 6:9–13 ESV

Jesus' exemplary prayer is commonly called the "Lord's Prayer." Some argue that it should be called the "disciples' prayer" since it was intended for Jesus' disciples. Or if you grew up Catholic, you referred to it as the "Our Father." I

(Steve) still remember with amazement my college room-mate reciting it so fast that you could hardly distinguish the words. In his Catholic background, reciting some "Our Fathers" was a common punishment (or requirement for penance), and he evidently had been punished frequently, thus acquiring his great skill.

This prayer is at the heart of the meaning of the Sermon. It resounds with the reoccurring themes of the two books we have co-written, as we have stressed (1) the corporate nature of the Kingdom and (2) the need to surrender to God's rule and God's will.

By the time of the Didache (a "teaching" on basic Christian practices anywhere from the late first century to the middle of the second century) people were encouraged to recite the Lord's Prayer three times a day, perhaps missing Jesus' whole point. But that is always the danger; along the way we can miss the point and turn a godly practice into rules and formulas that lose the principles. The key is to stay humble and open. We feel this challenge as we write this book.

Prayer from the Heart

So let's look again at the immediate context (Matthew 6:5–9) before we look at the prayer itself. To give us a more contemporary flavor, we will use *The Message* paraphrase:

> "And when you come before God, don't turn that into a theatrical production either. All these people making a regular show out of their prayers, hoping for stardom! Do you think God sits in a box seat?

> "Here's what I want you to do: Find a quiet, se-
> cluded place so you won't be tempted to role-play
> before God. Just be there as simply and honestly as
> you can manage. The focus will shift from you to
> God, and you will begin to sense his grace.
>
> "The world is full of so-called prayer warriors who
> are prayer-ignorant. They're full of formulas and pro-
> grams and advice, peddling techniques for getting
> what you want from God. Don't fall for that non-
> sense. This is your Father you are dealing with, and
> he knows better than you what you need. With a
> God like this loving you, you can pray very simply.
> Like this:"

So what is the point? Prayer is neither a show nor an exercise. It is not about me pleasing myself. An audience of one is still an audience.

The terrifying thing about Jesus' warning is not how bad the Pharisees were, but rather how deceptive and destructive sin is. It will boldly go with us into the presence of God and snatch away our souls even as we approach him. This warning is for us. Don't make the horrible mistake of thinking it is about someone else.

This leads us to a disclaimer: We don't write as those who think we have this all figured out. It feels presumptuous to talk about the Lord's Prayer at all, to talk about prayer at all. As we have studied, we kept thinking, "We need to stop preparing and spend our time praying." This is true for all of us, no matter what we may be doing.

Our Father

Note that prayer begins with a simple focus: God as Father. Who is God? Jesus' real answer to that question will take an eternity to understand, so for now let's just simply say "Father."

So why did Jesus choose to teach us to call God "Father"? We think because that is who we most need him to be. The world desperately needs to know a loving and compassionate father. Some of us have (or had) dads that we are very grateful for. They believe in us. They support us. They also tell us the truth, even if it's not what we want to hear. If we disappoint them, they love us anyway. If we struggle or fail, they remain a secure place where we can go. They encourage, they guide, and most of all they never abandon us. Sadly, not all fathers are like this, but those who are give us a little taste of who God, *the* Father, is. They resemble him, but they are not him. He is what they are but much more.

When we pray, Jesus says we come to a Father who cares. Speaking in Aramaic, he most likely would have used the word "Abba." He is saying that when we pray, we come to our *Papa*. The universe is not a cold, empty place after all, but a place to know your real dad. So how do we pray? We pray like little children talking to their father; this is the essence of prayer.

The word that comes before "Father" is the word "our." If any American had been teaching us to pray, it would have probably been "My Father." Individualism greatly shapes our thinking even about relating to God, and sometimes especially about relating to God. But the way Jesus teaches us to pray reminds us it is not just about "my" relationship with God, but about how we know God as a community or a fellowship. And so when we pray, we never really pray alone, even if we are in a secluded place and quite physically alone. We pray as a part of the kingdom people. We pray as one of the brothers and sisters. Who are we? His children. We belong to him and thus we belong to each other.

In Heaven

This God of ours is not on earth. He is not a human invention. He is so immense, so incredible, so awesome that our minds are not capable of grasping who he is. "Our Father" makes him real and touchable; it brings God down to our level, but the "who is in the heavens" (literally translated) makes sure we fully comprehend his Greatness, his Majesty, his "Otherness." We are talking to our Heavenly Father. The apostle Paul uses the expression "God and Father of our Lord Jesus Christ" frequently.

Let's remember that to pray to God we have to raise our view; we have to lift our eyes. We are limited by this earth, but he is not! If we miss this, then our prayers miss God.

Seven Petitions

Once we are clear about who we are talking to, we follow seven petitions in the prayer. The first three are parallel and concern *drawing near* to our Father: his *name*, his *Kingdom* and his *will*.

- May your name be holy.
- May your Kingdom come.
- May your will be done on earth as in heaven.

If the first part of the prayer is a call to *draw near*, it may be good to see the second part as a call to *bow down*. The next four petitions concern us and our needs, and the verbs are in the second person instead of the third person as in the first three.

- Give us this day our daily bread.
- Forgive us our debts as we have also forgiven our debtors.
- Lead us not into temptation.
- Deliver us from evil.

1. May your name be holy. The first petition is commonly translated, "Hallowed be thy name." What does that mean? "To be hallowed" or "to make holy" means "to sanctify, to set apart something as special." In other words, it is not common. This goes back to the nature of God. He is "other." He is special, valuable; thus it means "to honor," "to esteem," "to revere" or "to prize." The total opposite is "to profane," which means to take what is holy and treat it as plain and ordinary.

Remember that to the Jews God's covenant name was so special that they would not even speak it out loud. They referred to God as "the Name" to show great respect. The name of God is synonymous with God himself in all his power and glory. Notice this concept in Jesus' own prayer to the Father in John 17:

> "Holy Father, protect them by the power of your name—the name you gave me—so that they may be one as we are one. While I was with them, I protected them and kept them safe by that name you gave me." (vv11–12)

Where should this honoring be taking place? First and foremost in our hearts! And then through us into the whole world. How concerned are we about God's honor, about his glory? Are there things that we do that make God look bad in people's eyes? The kingdom person wants his words and actions to show God's name is holy.

2. May your Kingdom come. This, of course, is the essential prayer. This is crying out for the Kingdom that Jesus saw as his central message. "Your kingdom come." The Kingdom was always in his heart and on his tongue. It is the rule and the reign of the Lord in the hearts and lives of men. How many times have these three words been recited by those who had no idea of the revolutionary consequences?

This is a prayer of both personal submission and missionary zeal. We are being taught to pray for God's reign to come over our entire lives. It is the act of laying all our agendas—be they personal, financial, political or spiritual—before God in complete surrender to his agenda.

At the same time we are being taught to pray that his rule and reign will spread into the lives of many others. As long as men's hearts are not submitted to him, as long as anyone remains unaware of his honor and glory, work remains to be done. And it is our work, for we are all missionaries; we are all evangelists. We all need this passion, this zeal, this fervor to see the Kingdom come. To see the gospel spread.

Where are you praying the Kingdom will come? In your own heart? To your family? In your neighborhood? To your city?

3. May your will be done on earth as it is in heaven. We have an example here of Jewish parallelism. This second statement is parallel to the previous one—"Your kingdom come"—and restates it perhaps making it more personal. The Kingdom breaks into our lives when God's will is done on earth as it is in heaven. What is more personal than giving up what I want? At the same time it is clarifying its ultimate extension. The reign of God and the will of God come when God is ruling in all areas of our lives.

Are there areas of your life in which you are holding back? Not giving up control? Whenever we find ourselves saying to God, "You can have only this much and no more" or "I will only go this far and no farther," then we have lost sight of the Kingdom. To pray this prayer conscientiously, mindfully and sincerely is both socially and politically a radical act. It means declaring that your highest allegiance is not to your family or your culture or your nation, but to the place of your new citizenship—to heaven, to the Kingdom that comes from there and to the one who rules there.

When prayed from the heart, it is a dangerous and subversive prayer. It will lead us into conflict. The ways of the world and the ways of heaven don't have much in common; so when we pray "as it is in heaven," we are asking for trouble. If our prayer is genuine, trouble will find us.

This is the kind of trouble Jesus and those who followed him stirred up. It is amazing how upset people can get at someone who teaches us to be poor in spirit and meek, to use no oaths, not to resist an evil person, not to fight a lawsuit, to genuinely and seriously love our enemies, and to stop accumulating earthly treasure. When the ways of heaven come to earth, there is trouble.

But if you dare to live by faith and pray this prayer, hear with confidence some of Jesus last words: "I have told you these things, so that in me you may have peace. In this world you will have trouble. But take heart! I have overcome the world" (John 16:33).

Our whole focus should be living as citizens of heaven and keeping our eyes on heaven and the character of God. But we are not just waiting for the final revelation of the Kingdom (the "not yet"); we are living the Kingdom on earth right here and now. We are not just praying to "go to heaven when we die" but to live heaven now on earth before we die.

Now we go to the last four petitions. As we mentioned, the first three call us to draw near and the last four to bow down.

4. Give us this day our daily bread. "Bread" here refers to that which sustains life. While most people see this as praying for our daily necessities, David Scaer makes a strong case for the idea that while this may include physical bread and all it represents, the context and Jesus' other references to bread suggests that much more than the physical is in his mind. This is the spiritual bread needed to sustain the new kingdom life.[1]

The exact background and meaning of the next Greek word, "daily," is debated (surprisingly used only here and in Luke and not found in other Greek literature). The nature of the word (*epiousionis*) indicates a daily portion or necessary amount, but the idea is clear: It refers to what we need, our daily requirement, what is necessary.

We might ask why we should pray for something if God already knows we need it (as we will find out later in verse 32). God is love and he wants a daily relationship with us. We on the other hand desperately need a daily relationship with him. It is not optional. We need a relationship with our Father the way we need air to breathe. No air and we die. This is not at all like we "need" a Big Mac. No Big Mac and we are still alive. If we don't have a relationship with God, we are dead, spiritually dead.

As the Israelites needed the manna fresh every morning for their physical sustenance in the desert, we need Jesus, the bread of life, fresh every day to live this kingdom life in the midst of a world where we are aliens. So the kingdom person will face each new day saying, "Father, I am dependent on you. Give me what I need physically and spiritually, not for my own desires, but that your will might be lived out in me."

5. Forgive us our debts as we have also forgiven our debtors. Luke's account (11:2–4) contains the more familiar "sins" (rather than debts), but the word translated "debts" is more comprehensive, including the idea of "sins." In the context of kingdom thinking, with the Old Testament emphasis on the forgiveness of debts as an expression of justice to the poor, we should not rule out the idea that this is also in mind here.

The use of "our" is a reminder of many of the Old Testament prayers, such as in Nehemiah 1, for example, where men confessed and owned not only their own specific sins, but also the sins of their people throughout history. While this is not a common way of thinking in our day and age, it is one that we as disciples must still understand and practice.

"As we have also forgiven our debtors." Here the "we" emphasizes our need to forgive others as we look to God to forgive us. Who are "our debtors"? Think about all who have wronged you, who have hurt you, who "owe" you, whether love, respect, kindness, money or something else. Jesus thought this was so crucial that he continued speaking about it after the prayer was ended:

> "For if you forgive men when they sin against you, your heavenly Father will also forgive you. But if you do not forgive men their sins, your Father will not forgive your sins." (Matthew 6:14–15)

Again, by his repetition Jesus calls us to see just how important it is to forgive others. How many Christians are crippled by their inability to let go of hurts, to find peace with others, to be plagued by the past. Jesus teaches us that the only righteous path is the one of forgiveness.

6. *Lead us not into temptation.* This petition is clearly an admission of our weakness and our need. While we seek this new life in an old world, there will be efforts to pull us back toward the old in all kinds of ways. The disciple must find help from God to overcome.

The word ("tempt" or "test") is the same word that Paul uses in 1 Corinthians 10:13, where the Christian finds assurance about the strength that he can find:

> No temptation has seized you except what is common to man. And God is faithful; he will not let you be tempted beyond what you can bear. But when you are tempted, he will also provide a way out so that you can stand up under it.

When our humanity seems to get the best of us, we can find direction in the words Jesus spoke to his disciples in the garden in Matthew 26:41:

> "Watch and pray so that you will not fall into temptation. The spirit is willing, but the body is weak."

To pray this part of the prayer helps us to know where we are vulnerable. As you consider the call to kingdom living, what are some of the temptations that you see now but maybe did not see before these thoughts about the Sermon were presented to you? Your prayers about those will be crucial.

7. *Deliver us from evil.* Amazingly, a search of the Internet reveals that this phrase may be the most popular one in the prayer. One finds dozens of references to it on various secular websites before there's any reference to it in traditional religious contexts. The phrase is everywhere.

For a people who seem good at ignoring God or giving him only lip service, we still have an obsession with evil and some sense of needing deliverance from it.

The problem is we are mistaken about where it comes from in its most dangerous forms. We think it comes from rouge nations, as in the "axis of evil." We think it is something we escape by keeping the wrong people off airplanes. We are shocked when it shows up in the child pornographer or meth dealer right in our own neighborhood. In other words, for most people, evil is something "out there."

But when Jesus says, "Deliver us from evil," he connects it with temptations that come within each of us. To those who think it is primarily "out there," like 90% of us probably do, here are Jesus' mind-changing words:

> "But the things that come out of the mouth come from the heart, and these make a man 'unclean.' For out of the heart come evil thoughts, murder, adultery, sexual immorality, theft, false testimony, slander." (Matthew 15:18–19)

Evil is not so much "out there" as it is "in here" (and we are pointing at ourselves). We believe it is in the spirit of this prayer to cry, "Help us, O Father, with temptation, and deliver us from the evil in our own heart. And, Father, deliver us first from the fiction that evil is not really our problem."

Some translations read "evil one" and although that is possible, it would limit the scope of the idea for there is evil in all of us lurking in our hearts, seeking for an opportunity to rebel as Satan did against our only true Lord and Master.

Why should we pray this? Because we don't want our fellowship with our Father to be broken! There is a spiritual battle. We are in it. It rages all around us.

In all recent translations the prayer ends with the seventh petition. In the King James Version, the prayer ends with this familiar quote: "For thine is the kingdom, and the power, and the glory, forever. Amen."

Although this doxology was not found in the earliest manuscripts, it definitely represents a very early addition at a time when the prayer was included in the public worship of the church. And as we pray the prayer, these words, fitting well with the spirit of Jesus' message, add a fitting climax.

A Heart to Pray

Jesus began this teaching that we have looked at by saying, "Pray then like this." Jesus is not only saying we should pray; he is also saying there is a way to pray. But let us be careful here. This does not mean that there is a formula or a mantra to repeat. It means there is a heart to have.

- A heart of warmth and family (Our Father)
- A heart of respect (hallowed be your name)
- A heart of submission (your kingdom come)
- A heart of surrender (your will be done)
- A heart of dependency (give us today our daily bread)
- A heart of humility and brokenness (forgive us our debts)
- A heart of gratitude (as we forgive our debtors)
- A heart of self-examination (lead us not into temptation and deliver us from evil)

Do we hear Jesus? We need to pray. We need to pray just like we need to breathe. Some people are spiritually oxygen-deprived. They are trying to be human and real and alive without prayer. How sad. We need to pray.

Step Out

And as we end our prayer, having *drawn near* and having *bowed down*, we now *step out*.

- We step out *in faith*.
- We step out *in love*.
- We step out *with a newfound vision* of who God is and who we are and how things should be in this world.

Draw near. Bow down. Step out.

Questions for Study and Discussion

1. Why would you say prayer is so central to kingdom living, and why did it make so much sense for Jesus to include it in the Sermon?
2. Go through the material on each of the seven petitions asking yourself what difficulties you may encounter and where your heart is on each of them.
3. Why is it important to be praying daily for the Kingdom to come (to "break in") to our lives and the lives of our faith family?
4. What are some teachings you have studied in this book so far that you know you need to be praying about?

20
Kingdom Treasure

"Do not store up for yourselves treasures on earth, where moth and rust destroy, and where thieves break in and steal. But store up for yourselves treasures in heaven, where moth and rust do not destroy, and where thieves do not break in and steal. For where your treasure is, there your heart will be also."

Matthew 6:19–21

When the two of us first began our joint exploration of Jesus' kingdom teaching, we almost immediately realized that our greatest challenge would be what this message says about our earthly possessions. Even though both of us have sought for years to have a biblical perspective in regard to money and earthly "stuff," reading afresh Jesus' teaching and the thoughts of other spiritual thinkers caused us to realize that our hearts had to be open to going much further.

Having taught us to seek the Kingdom especially through prayer, Jesus now zeros in on those things that often preoccupy our minds and hearts. More literally verse 19 could be translated "Treasure not up for yourselves treasures on earth.... But treasure for yourselves treasures in heaven." Jesus is targeting our hearts, our mindset: What do we treasure; what do we find valuable; what do we feel is most significant?

And then he says something that may surprise us a bit: "For where your treasure is there your heart will be also." We may have expected him to speak first about the heart and to say "where your heart is there your treasure will be also." And that, of course, would be true.

But he lets us know that wherever we invest our time, energies and money will inevitably lead our heart to follow to that place. If we invest heavily in treasures on earth, our heart will follow our investment. We will have a "vested" interest in those things.

On the other hand, if we invest heavily in treasures in heaven, our hearts will grow more and more attached to that investment. If we decide to put our treasures in heaven, no matter what we are feeling, our hearts will ultimately follow that decision.

When we give generously to the church to support its mission and to individuals to help them with their lives, our hearts go to a good place, and we are more and more freed from our attachment to material things. This is a freedom that we desperately need.

Our Spiritual Eye

If Jesus' teaching here is about the heart, it is also about the eyes. We hear him go on to say,

> "The eye is the lamp of the body. If your eyes are good, your whole body will be full of light. But if your eyes are bad, your whole body will be full of darkness. If then the light within you is darkness, how great is that darkness!
>
> "No one can serve two masters. Either he will hate the one and love the other, or he will be devoted to the one and despise the other. You cannot serve both God and Money." (Matthew 6:22–24)

How you live and what you go after in life has to do with the spiritual eye. If we basically see life through the right lenses, our life will be full of light. The word "good" ("if your eyes are good") is sometimes rendered "healthy" or "clear." Literally it is the word for "single" and not a word that is normally used to refer to the eye unless to describe blurred or double vision. (As an aside, maybe this is why at the place of judgment there will be weeping and the gnashing of teeth as many will finally see clearly what they refused to see in life.)

If we see life accurately through the eyes of heaven, then our whole life will be full of light. However, if our view of life is wrong, our lives will be filled with darkness. For Jesus this is a matter of mastery. In other words: Your choice of master will determine the clarity of your vision. Different translations word the choice differently:

- NIV: God and Money
- NASB: God and Wealth
- KJV: God and Mammon

Money and Possessions

The word is *mamōna* and has a Semitic origin that refers to wealth, riches and possessions. It stands for all our earthly things that we can look to for security. And as Jesus sees it, mammon competes robustly for control of our eyes, lives and thoughts. On one hand, Jesus knew that in this world money and possessions are needed—to some extent. We can see from the generosity of disciples in the New Testament churches that money can be used for much good.

However, one cannot read Jesus' teaching carefully and fail to see that, at the same time, *money is dangerous.* Do we hear this alarm? There is a force at work here that struggles against God, and it seeks to master us. Unless we are vigilant, it will do just that.

Jesus' strong message was certainly carried on to the early church, as we see in this statement from Paul in 1 Timothy 6:6–10:

> But godliness with contentment is great gain. For we brought nothing into the world, and we can take nothing out of it. But if we have food and clothing, we will be content with that. People who want to get rich fall into temptation and a trap and into many foolish and harmful desires that plunge men into ruin and destruction. For the love of money is a root of all kinds of evil. Some people, eager for

> money, have wandered from the faith and pierced
> themselves with many griefs.

While we have appreciation for courses in Christian financial management that emphasize responsibility and freedom from debt, we are often disturbed by a parallel message that says, "It is fine to want to be rich." One radio personality puts it this way: "Have piles and piles of cash." Paul's statement could not be clearer: "People who want to get rich fall into temptation and a trap...." We may start out with good motives, but piles and piles of cash can do something to our hearts. It is not a coincidence that we find the words "love" and "money" in numerous biblical texts, always accompanied by a strong warning of danger. With this matter of mastery on the table, we will have to make numerous conscious decisions not to locate treasures on earth.

There is a caveat here: No one can say for someone else "how much is enough." If someone is concerned about where our hearts are, we welcome their feedback because any of us can be deceived. However, in the final analysis each of us must work out our own hearts before God. We cannot tell you the size house you need, the type of vehicle you should drive or the type of retirement plan you should have. But we can say that kingdom people will not approach any of this the way it is ordinarily approached in the world. As ambassadors of Christ, it must be clear that we are treasuring treasures in heaven.

Do Not Worry

A focus on money is not to be a part of the kingdom life, but Jesus also makes it clear that something else does not belong: *worry*. Here is the rest of Chapter 6:

> "Therefore I tell you, do not worry about your life, what you will eat or drink; or about your body, what you will wear. Is not life more important than food, and the body more important than clothes? Look at the birds of the air; they do not sow or reap or store away in barns, and yet your heavenly Father feeds them. Are you not much more valuable than they? Who of you by worrying can add a single hour to his life?
>
> "And why do you worry about clothes? See how the lilies of the field grow. They do not labor or spin. Yet I tell you that not even Solomon in all his splendor was dressed like one of these. If that is how God clothes the grass of the field, which is here today and tomorrow is thrown into the fire, will he not much more clothe you, O you of little faith? So do not worry, saying, 'What shall we eat?' or 'What shall we drink?' or 'What shall we wear?' For the pagans run after all these things, and your heavenly Father knows that you need them. But seek first his kingdom and his righteousness, and all these things will be given to you as well. Therefore do not worry about tomorrow, for tomorrow will worry about itself. Each day has enough trouble of its own." (Matthew 6:20–34)

We might not all be eager to be rich, but we do all strug-gle precisely at the points Jesus addresses here. We worry. We fret. We awfulize. We catastrophize. We think, "What about this?" and "What if that happens?" or "What if this doesn't come through?" Never mind that we know worry does no good; we have this sense that if we don't worry, we somehow aren't being diligent or aren't paying attention or aren't caring.

However, we need to again appreciate how starkly Jesus puts things. Worry is pagan. It is a pagan quality. It's not just a bad habit. It is not just a little character flaw. It is a denial of God's sovereignty, God's concern and God's commitment to us. We should deal with it as forcefully as we deal with lust. When the lustful thought appears in our minds, we must say, "No. That is not who I am, and I will not go there." In the same way when worry springs to our minds, we must marshal weapons of righteousness in the right hand and left and drive it out, saying clearly, "This does not fit with my life under the reign and rule of God."

Worry is a declaration of fear and quite the opposite of a declaration of faith. Just as we may not ever be able to stop lustful temptations from appearing on the screens of our minds, we will likely always have some instinct to worry. But we must shout back and drive out those voices, seeing them as completely inconsistent with God's rule and reign.

Seek First

At the end Jesus gives the ultimate antidote to worry and perhaps the ultimate expression of kingdom living: "Seek first his kingdom and his righteousness, and all these things will be given to you as well" (Matthew 6:33). We could have subtitled this chapter "The Simple Life" because in this one verse Jesus makes it all very simple. All we have to do is bring ourselves before God, pray for his will to be done in our lives on earth as it is in heaven—that is, seek first the kingdom—and then God works and accomplishes the rest.

We would recommend Vernard Eller's book *The Simple Life,* in which he says there are only two things: that which is "first" and then "all the rest." The "first" is our decision and "all the rest" is provided by God. Learning to know the difference between the "first" and "all the rest" makes all the difference.[1]

Questions for Study and Discussion

1. We all have to live in this world and have physical possessions just to function. What is the difference between this and "storing up treasures on earth"?
2. What are some steps you can take to cut yourself free from the culture of conspicuous consumption that many of us find ourselves in?
3. Why is worry so much at odds with kingdom-seeking?

21
Kingdom Judgments

"Do not judge, or you too will be judged. For in the same way you judge others, you will be judged, and with the measure you use, it will be measured to you.

"Why do you look at the speck of sawdust in your brother's eye and pay no attention to the plank in your own eye? How can you say to your brother, 'Let me take the speck out of your eye,' when all the time there is a plank in your own eye? You hypocrite, first take the plank out of your own eye, and then you will see clearly to remove the speck from your brother's eye.

"Do not give dogs what is sacred; do not throw your pearls to pigs. If you do, they may trample them under their feet, and then turn and tear you to pieces."

Matthew 7:1–6

As we turn to this passage, we find ourselves dealing with another text that has been often quoted but often misused. We should start out by realizing that judging others is very much a part of our human nature, just like lust and worry. For some of us it is a deep-seated character trait. Early in my life I (Steve) realized that I was a very critical and judgmental person. In high school I became interested in journalism and admired writers and editors who were able to take people apart with their words. So Jesus' words here challenge me on a deeply personal level.

We are talking about kingdom living. This is a totally new way to live, to handle life; it is Jesus' way; it is the kingdom way.

A Judgmental Spirit

What does Jesus mean by "do not judge"? To understand the text more clearly, we will quote R.V.G. Tasker:[1]

> The form of the prohibition in verse 1 (*krinete* followed by the present imperative) makes it clear that it is the habit of censorious and carping criticism that Jesus is condemning. The present tense gives it that sense of continuing or constant criticism, so then it could be translated: "don't be continually judgmental (or critical)."

The verb *krinete* or "judge" is used only three times in Matthew. Besides the use here it is used in a legal sense in 5:40 and regarding the final judgment in 19:28.

So let's use our imagination. Picture yourself in a courtroom. Maybe you've never personally been in one, but we've all seen them on television. So when you're in the courtroom, where is the judge? Above the rest, right? He is seated on a raised platform behind a large desk looking down on the one to be judged.

To me that imagery helps capture what Jesus is saying. Don't be the judge. Don't sit in judgment. Don't put yourself in the position of looking down on others with a critical heart and attitude.

Obviously Jesus is not saying don't have opinions, even less don't express them. For example, what we find in verses 6 and 15 definitely require some discernment, some "judgment."

> "Do not give dogs what is sacred; do not throw your pearls to pigs. If you do, they may trample them under their feet, and then turn and tear you to pieces." (Matthew 7:6)

> "Watch out for false prophets. They come to you in sheep's clothing, but inwardly they are ferocious wolves. By their fruit you will recognize them. Do people pick grapes from thornbushes, or figs from thistles?" (Matthew 7:15–16)

These passages make it clear that Jesus expects us to utilize our capacity to discern and make the right kind of judgments about others. He is not saying don't notice people's faults. He is not saying ignore their sins. He is definitely teaching us that we should help our brothers and sisters.

What is consistent with everything else we have seen so far in the Sermon is the idea that Jesus is teaching us not to be self-righteous and not to see ourselves as above others.

At the risk of being too repetitive, we say again, one of the great dangers in our response to Jesus' call to a deeper commitment, to a higher standard of righteousness, to living out this kingdom life, is self-righteousness. We can commit ourselves to his high calling and then start to look down on those who have not (1) made the same commitments we have made or (2) made the same decisions about what commitment looks like.

So we have to go back to the Beatitudes. Back to wrestling with being poor in spirit. We have to see ourselves as God does. He is the only judge. Before we can help others, Jesus is telling us that we first have to deal with ourselves, that we have to be open about our own struggles as we try to help others with theirs.

True Spirituality

In much of the Sermon we find Jesus contrasting true spirituality, true relationships with the way of life of the Pharisees and the religious experts. What we have found is the longer we try to follow Jesus and put into practice his teachings, the more easily we fall into the very things he so strongly opposes. If we do not fight our sinful nature to be judgmental and critical, then we will find ourselves becoming the biggest Pharisees.

Do we have the tendency to see others' sin as bigger, as

worse, as more sinful than our own? Do we find ourselves thinking, "How can he call himself a Christian and do *that*?"

No Hypocrisy

Another thing that Jesus is teaching here is that we are not to be hypocritical. So he uses this funny story—or maybe it is really a scary story. He tells us about a person who sees his brother struggling with the speck of dust in his eye, and he wants to help. What's wrong with that? Well the problem is person number one has a plank sticking out of his eye. For the older baseball fans among us, imagine a guy with a Louisville Slugger protruding from his eye. We can imagine the difficulty when "bat guy" tries to help the guy with the speck.

Jesus says to him, "You hypocrite." If we dress up our criticism as kindness (in that we just want to help), this does not change the nature of our critical heart, of our judgmental nature. What Jesus is saying is that we *first* have to deal with ourselves—our weakness and our sins—so that we will be able to actually help our brother, our friend. When we do not deal with our own hearts, even our best efforts at helping others become bumbling attempts that may do more harm than good.

Love One Another

Most of all Jesus is teaching us how to love one another. Remember that the "righteousness" that Jesus calls us to is primarily "right relationships." We have got to be involved in each other's lives. When we are and we see flaws (and when we are more involved we will see more flaws!), we cannot sit back with folded arms in judgment on each other. We must "get in there" and be an active and loving part of their life and their spiritual growth.

Jesus says, "First take the log of your own eye, and then you will see clearly to take the speck out of your brother's eye." He is clearly calling us to help our brother, but first to deal with ourselves.

You see, there are no "armchair quarterbacks," no "Monday morning coaches." We are all in the game; nobody is on the sidelines. Maybe you have been hurt and on the sidelines for a while, but that is not where Jesus wants you to stay. He wants all of us to be in the game. And the game is all about helping each other. It is about loving one another

We both grew up in the Southern United States where the people have a reputation for good old Southern hospitality. Our experience is that in order to practice this "hospitality," people sometimes substitute niceness for honesty. All of us, Southern and otherwise, can be so afraid of hurting someone's feelings that we don't give helpful input.

Jesus is calling us to a "kingdom culture," to a way of thinking that is more influenced by the ways of heaven than by the ways of men on earth.

Speak the Truth in Love

We are probably all familiar with the story of "The Emperor's New Clothes." You have the emperor with all of his cohorts and advisers, and nobody is willing to tell him the truth. It takes a child to blurt out, "The emperor has no clothes," to awaken everybody to the reality that no one was willing to see.

We have to "speak the truth in love" as Paul said in Ephesians 4:15. The challenge is to build a culture of honesty and truth in an environment of love. That is what we need to find in our fellowship. To accomplish this we will all have to really work at it together!

You have probably noticed that some sports teams publically criticize the one who messed up. Then there are other teams that encourage the one who messed up and then privately help him not make the same mistake again. This is what we are supposed to be—a team where we are all pulling together and helping each other not to keep making the same mistakes.

This is huge: We have to want help and to accept help if we are going to be able to help each other. As I (Steve) have personally dealt with my critical nature, it has been impossible to make lasting changes without help from others. Of course, my wife, Diane, who has probably borne the brunt of my judgmental nature, has been a great help. My friend Tom will gently call my attention to my tendency to slide back into old habits of criticism and negativity. Thank God for them. I need help to grow and change. We all do. That's why God put us in the church. That's what church is all about—helping us be more like Jesus.

The only vertical relationships in the kingdom are between

us and God; all other relationships are horizontal—brother to brother, sister to sister, brother to sister. Even when we are sharing our faith with someone and helping them to study the Bible, we should have mutual respect and love.

When we love people, we will want to know their circumstances and their background so we can better understand who they are and why they do what they do. Only then can we offer the most sensitive and helpful input. And obviously we want to be open so we can be known by others as well.

Careful Judgments

Before we close this chapter, let's look briefly at verses 2 and 6. What Jesus tells us here is particularly sobering: "For in the same way you judge others, you will be judged, and with the measure you use, it will be measured to you." This doesn't need much commentary. We must be very careful with the way we look at others and the judgments we make. These judgments (or discernments) need to be based on facts, but more than that, they need to be filled with grace and guided by love. And this is what we are grateful to receive from God—a whole lot of grace and a whole lot of love.

The teaching in verse 6, "Do not give dogs what is sacred; do not throw your pearls to pigs. If you do, they may trample them under their feet, and then turn and tear you to pieces" needs to be handled with great caution. In the spirit of dealing with your own heart first and not judging, we should be very slow in assigning people to the categories of "dogs" and "pigs."

We cannot, however, ignore what Jesus plainly says. There are situations when we have done all we can, when we have been as patient as possible, and when we just need to move on. One application I can see of this applies to studying the Bible with people. When a person is not responding to the Word, when they are not taking it seriously, continuing trying to move forward may do more harm than good.

No Judgmental Attitudes

We want to conclude this chapter by challenging you to make a decision to treat judging just like lust and worry. Get it out of your life.

You might try this exercise to make you aware of just how much of a problem it is for you. Take a 3" x 5" card with you for the next week, and write down every time you find yourself judging someone.

- A co-worker
- A fellow church member
- A politician
- A member of another church

And ask yourself, "Is this judgment hypocritical or righteous? Am I being self-righteous? Is this judgment made with or without facts? Is it based on prejudice? Do I know everything that is going on?"

After you do this, share what you found out about yourself with another person who will commit to remind you when you're falling back into your judgmental and critical ways.

Questions for Study and Discussion

1. What are clearly some wrong ways to apply Jesus' statement, "Do not judge"?
2. How does a judgmental spirit manifest itself in a person's life? Give some examples.
3. How does this most challenge you?
4. How is speaking the truth in love very different from the attitude that Jesus condemns?

22

Kingdom Confidence

"Ask and it will be given to you; seek and you will find; knock and the door will be opened to you. For everyone who asks receives; he who seeks finds; and to him who knocks, the door will be opened.

"Which of you, if his son asks for bread, will give him a stone? Or if he asks for a fish, will give him a snake? If you, then, though you are evil, know how to give good gifts to your children, how much more will your Father in heaven give good gifts to those who ask him! So in everything, do to others what you would have them do to you, for this sums up the Law and the Prophets."

Matthew 7:7–12

As we have already noted, the kingdom life cannot be lived without prayer. Now we come to the second major section in the Sermon where Jesus emphasizes the importance of prayer, and in this case, gives assurances that it will be heard and will have power. The fact that Jesus uses three present imperatives—ask, seek and knock—would seem to stress three aspects of prayer: (1) the type of urgency that a disciple should have in coming to God, (2) the humble nature to be demonstrated when we come, and (3) the way in which we are to continue to come again and again.

Jesus' use of three words with essentially the same meaning seems to be done to first emphasize urgency. As disciples we are in a state of need, and we need to be actively searching for God's help in every possible way. Additionally, each of these words describes what we do when we realize we will not find the answers or the resources on our own power. And finally, since the words in Greek are in the present imperative, which implies continuous action, there is the idea of "keep on asking,""keep on seeking," "keep on knocking." Since there is something worth finding, Jesus urges us to demonstrate persistence. In Luke's Gospel this teaching is connected with the following story:

> Then he said to them, "Suppose one of you has a friend, and he goes to him at midnight and says, 'Friend, lend me three loaves of bread, because a friend of mine on a journey has come to me, and I have nothing to set before him.'
>
> "Then the one inside answers, 'Don't bother me. The door is already locked, and my children are with me in bed. I can't get up and give you anything.'
>
> "I tell you, though he will not get up and give him the bread because he is his friend, yet because

of the man's boldness he will get up and give him
as much as he needs." (Luke 11:5–8)

Jesus is not teaching that God is reluctant to give. This
is clear from Matthew 7:9–11 and Luke 11:11–13. The message is that we need to be persistent in seeking.

Prayer to Live the Kingdom Life

However, as we have emphasized in earlier chapters, it
is important to take note of the context before we make an
application from a biblical passage. There are promises here
that can give disciples great confidence when they pray, but
what is it that we are to be asking for? What is it we are to
be seeking? What is it we hope to find on the other side of
the door?

In our experience, we believe this passage is seldom
looked at in context. We have just heard Jesus give some of
the most revolutionary teachings that can be imagined, and
this statement must have something to do with what he has
said up to this point. Isn't it true that these teachings challenge us to the core? In some cases don't they leave us per-
plexed, wondering just how to make application of them to
real life? Isn't it true that all kinds of people get this far in
the Sermon on the Mount and throw their hands up, feeling
this is an impossible calling? In such a context, isn't Jesus
telling us that if we will passionately and persistently seek
answers with a heart to obey, we will find what we seek?

We don't want to suggest that there are no other applications of this passage. Indeed, it occurs in a slightly different

context in Luke's Gospel. However, it is interesting in the contemporary church how often the statements here are applied to such things as seeking a spouse, asking for health or finding a job without even considering that Jesus is first of all telling us to pursue answers to some issues related to kingdom living and to seek the power to courageously live what is revealed.

In a culture like ours, how do we overcome the temptation to lust? Amid some of our marriage and divorce complexities, how do we obey Jesus' teaching? How do we put into practice his teaching about nonresistance? What are the implications of truly loving our enemies in a way that is extraordinary among men?

It seems to us that Jesus is promising that those who keep on asking and keep on seeking and keep on knocking will find God's answers to these questions and will find the strength that comes from him to live out his will on earth as it is in heaven.

And so, if we are more persistent in asking for health than we are for the strength to be non-violent and loving toward enemies, we are off track. If we are more eager to pray for a job than we are to ask God's help to judge righteously, we are missing the depth of Jesus' teaching. If we are more proactive in seeking a spouse than we are in wanting to learn how to be reconciled to our brothers or how to handle our finances in kingdom ways, then something is amiss.

Let us notice that just eight verses before this passage begins, we have the other occasion in the Sermon when we are told to "seek." In 6:33 we are told to "seek first his King-dom." Isn't that what we need to keep on asking for? Isn't that what we need to keep on seeking? Don't we need to keep knocking so the door will be opened to us to give us power to live the kingdom life?

Trust God to Answer

However, if part of the thrust here is to encourage us to be active in seeking, Jesus is giving equal emphasis to the fact that we can completely trust God to respond to our requests. The illustration he uses of the father and his children communicates the idea that no normal father will mockingly respond to his children's legitimate requests. If a child asks for bread, will an earthly father give him a stone? It has been suggested that some of the stones on the banks of the Sea of Galilee resembled small loaves of bread. Would a father cruelly give his son something that looked like bread but would break his teeth? If his son asks for a fish—something that would provide nourishment, would his father give him a reptile that would cause him harm?

The assumption is that everyone would answer, "No!" But then Jesus says, "If you, then, though you are evil, know how to give good gifts to your children, how much more will your Father in heaven give good gifts to those who ask him?"

Did Jesus give us these teachings in the Sermon just to make us feel guilty? If we seek to eat this bread of life, will God give us a stone? No, these teachings describe the glori-ous life of the age to come, and if we are earnestly seeking to live this life, God will not mock our prayers. Indeed, we will experience what Vernard Eller calls "the much more of the Heavenly Father."

Just as we are to show the world the *perrison*—the "extraordinary" the "much more"—God will show the *perrison* to us. We will seek first the kingdom life, and God will generously give us the direction and power to live it. This will not bring us ruin, but will bring us the abundant life that Jesus came to impart.

The parallel passage in Luke says God will give us the Holy Spirit (Luke 11:13). This is further evidence that what God wants to give in response to our requests is the direction and the power for the kingdom life. The "good gifts" from him may not be the gifts we often envision within our natural mind, but rather gifts that are spiritually discerned.

So, let us be poor in spirit; let us admit our spiritual bankruptcy; let us confess that these age-to-come teachings are impossible for us—that in many cases they are impossible even for the natural man to comprehend. However, let us respond with meekness and humility to Jesus' call for us to ask, to seek and to knock. Let us stop whining about how hard these teachings are, and let us start living with faith in "the much more of the Heavenly Father."

Let us embrace the fact that when we ask, we will receive; and when we seek, we will find; and when we knock, the door to a dynamic kingdom life will be opened to us.

Questions for Study and Discussion

1. Why is it important to keep Jesus' teaching about asking and seeking and knocking in the context of the Sermon?

2. What does Jesus say in this text that should give us great confidence? How should that confidence affect us?

3. When Jesus gives this teaching in Matthew, he says, "If you, then, though you are evil, know how to give good gifts to your children, how much more will your Father in heaven give good gifts to those who ask him!" (Matthew 7:11). In Luke's account of similar teaching Jesus says, "If you then, though you are evil, know how to give good gifts to your children, how much more will your Father in heaven give the Holy Spirit to those who ask him!" (Luke 11:13). Discuss the similarities and the differences in the two accounts.

4. How should we be affected by "the much more of the Heavenly Father" as we seek to live the kingdom life?

23
The Kingdom Few

"Enter through the narrow gate. For wide is the gate and broad is the road that leads to destruction, and many enter through it. But small is the gate and narrow the road that leads to life, and only a few find it.

"Watch out for false prophets. They come to you in sheep's clothing, but inwardly they are ferocious wolves. By their fruit you will recognize them. Do people pick grapes from thornbushes, or figs from thistles? Likewise every good tree bears good fruit, but a bad tree bears bad fruit. A good tree cannot bear bad fruit, and a bad tree cannot bear good fruit.

"Every tree that does not bear good fruit is cut down and thrown into the fire. Thus, by their fruit you will recognize them.

"Not everyone who says to me, 'Lord, Lord,' will enter the Kingdom of heaven, but only he who does the will of my Father who is in heaven.

"Many will say to me on that day, 'Lord, Lord, did we not prophesy in your name, and in your name drive out demons and perform many miracles?'

"Then I will tell them plainly, 'I never knew you. Away from me, you evildoers!'"

Matthew 7:14–23

A s we come to the end of the Sermon, Jesus makes it clear that those who accept his message and put it into practice will be few in comparison to the many that will prefer a more natural, more intuitive and much easier way to travel. The idea that there are two paths was not new to Judaism, but Jesus goes on to give this teaching a distinctive emphasis.

There is a wide gate followed by the broad road. It is the path of least resistance. Traveling it requires little effort and minimal commitment. Self-discipline and self-denial are not required. You will be able to do plenty of coasting, and perseverance need not be a part of your character. This may sound like freedom and fun, and there will be times when it is. However, if it sounds too good to be true, it is! It has a major downside: It leads to destruction.

The other road begins with a narrow gate. It is not wide enough to accommodate all your stuff. There is much that will have to be left behind—mainly your "self." Humility and surrender are expected from the very beginning. Perhaps we should think of the Beatitudes as the narrow gate and the rest of the Sermon as the narrow way. Once through the gate, you do not find that the way gets broader. The challenges continue. The travels will not all be uphill, but times of coasting will be few and far between. On this road you have to really believe something; you have to be willing to sacrifice for it, and you have to be determined to persevere when the going is difficult.

This way is not hell, but it is hard. However, the upside is enormous: This is the way to life. And this life is not just something that comes when you reach the destination; it is experienced all along the way in the high times and even in the low times.

Choose Destruction or Life

There is quite a contrast between destruction and life. On the day that I (Tom) wrote much of this chapter I drove through parts of my home state of Alabama that were devastated by record-setting tornadoes eleven days earlier. I went there to try to be somewhat in touch with what people were going through and to try to offer some encouragement. The level of destruction was staggering. In one of the small towns thirty of thirty-one businesses were destroyed.

I saw front steps leading up to…nothing. Two weeks before, children may have gotten off school buses and dashed up those steps to their homes, saying, "Mom, we're home," but now there was nothing, not even rubble. It was as though the houses had vaporized. Three of those schoolchildren in that small town lost their lives.

For miles there was destruction. Schools, homes, church

buildings, businesses—all in ruins. But then one could drive a few more miles and once again see beautiful rolling hills, "earth's verdant glory" and the "blooming garb of spring."

The contrast between destruction and life was dramatic. Destruction is hard on the eyes and hard on the heart. Life is vibrant and full and inspiring. But there is no denying what Jesus said: Only a few will find it.

Only a Few

It is quite remarkable that only a few will find life. When surveys are taken in the United States, pollsters find that most people believe in heaven and believe that they are going there. A 2005 poll by ABC News found that 89% of those polled believe there is a heaven, and 85% believe they will be there. A year earlier a Gallup poll found that 77% of those questioned thought they had a very good chance of going to heaven. Either Jesus is wrong, or a lot of people are in for a big surprise. One is reminded of a line from an old spiritual song: "Everybody talking about heaven ain't going there."

What would be Jesus' motivation for saying only a few will find life? Perhaps we get an answer to this in the parallel passage in Luke's Gospel.

> Then Jesus went through the towns and villages, teaching as he made his way to Jerusalem. Someone asked him, "Lord, are only a few people going to be saved?"
>
> He said to them, "Make every effort to enter

> through the narrow door, because many, I tell you,
> will try to enter and will not be able to."
> (Luke 13:22–24)

Jesus wants the man to know how few are going to enter so he will be motivated to make every effort to be one of those few. God takes no pleasure in the death of anyone (Ezekiel 18:32).

"Winning the world for Jesus" has a noble sound to it, but while every effort should be made to take the gospel of the Kingdom to the ends of the earth, we must realize that this way of the Kingdom will be accepted only by a minority. How few? No one can say. However, most people will either find the message too radical or their love for God too little, and they will go away to destruction. It is a sad and sobering thought. The fact that so few will be saved is not due to a lack of love and compassion on God's part, but to hubris, self-will and rebellion on man's part.

The parallel passage in Luke referred to earlier continues with this story:

> "Once the owner of the house gets up and closes the door, you will stand outside knocking and pleading, 'Sir, open the door for us.'
>
> "But he will answer, 'I don't know you or where you come from.'
>
> "Then you will say, 'We ate and drank with you, and you taught in our streets.'
>
> "But he will reply, 'I don't know you or where you come from. Away from me, all you evildoers!'"
> (Luke 13:25–27)

This, of course, echoes Jesus' words in Matthew 7 where we hear him say,

> "Many will say to me on that day, 'Lord, Lord, did we not prophesy in your name, and in your name drive out demons and perform many miracles?' Then I will tell them plainly, 'I never knew you. Away from me, you evildoers!'"

What strikes us is the repetition of the word "many." *Many* will travel the broad road. *Many* will answer the poll question about heaven in the affirmative. It would seem that many who are on the broad road either think that it leads to life or that they are actually on the narrow road. In either case, they will be confronted with stunning words of rejection. Jesus never knew them.

Living Heaven Now

As we have contended in Volume One and now repeat in this volume, the Kingdom is made up of people who don't just want to go to heaven when they die, but want to live heaven and heaven's principles now on earth before they die. To those on the broad way (and a wrong way), it is enough to believe in heaven, talk about heaven and engage in token religion, but never take seriously what the Kingdom means—the reign and rule of God. Jesus never knew them.

Some of us with humble and obedient hearts, but with an accused makeup, may think, "That will likely be me."

Others of us with a prideful spirit and no hunger for righteousness, and yet an excused makeup, may think, "That could not possibly be me." In words drawn from Paul's statement in Romans 12, each of us should have a sober judgment of ourselves in the context of God's grace. Who will be saved? Who will be among the few? Only the humble—those humble enough to trust God's grace and those humble enough to admit how much they need it, and most of all those (whatever their natural makeup) humble enough to be changed by God's grace.

Lord, Lord

"Not everyone who says to me, 'Lord, Lord,' will enter the kingdom of heaven, but only he who does the will of my Father who is in heaven" (Matthew 7:21). Surely Jesus is using hyperbole here. Surely he doesn't mean this. Would he actually send away those who called him "Lord," those who prayed a prayer to him, those who did deeds in his name, those who were baptized in his name?

Yes, it appears he means what he says and is not using a scare tactic. He is not some Dali Lama-type figure who smiles and makes everyone feel they are okay. He is preaching the Kingdom of God, and those who do not put themselves under God's reign need to understand that religious actions and rhetoric are no substitute for humility, submission and obedience.

But what is this "will of my Father" he is talking about here? Again, it is critical to consider the context. This does not refer to our favorite doctrine or to something we are sure we have done that gives us reassurance, but enables us to hammer someone else. In this context, "the will of my Father" is nothing less than the message of the Sermon. Could it have a broader application? Yes, but we must hear it first and foremost in this context.

False Prophets

The false prophets referred to in verses 15–20 must be those who tamper with this message, who lead people to believe that something less than submission to the reign of God is good enough. These are not people who make some honest mistakes. Jesus says internally they are like ravenous wolves. The word in Greek is *harpax,* and if it has a sinister sound, that's appropriate, for it can refer to a robber or an extortioner. Biblically speaking, a false teacher is not just someone who is wrong, but someone with a character problem (see 1 Timothy 1:3–5).

It is likely that the false prophets Jesus speaks of are like those in Jeremiah's day; "They dress the wound of [the] people as though it were not serious. 'Peace, peace,' they say, when there is no peace" (Jeremiah 8:11). They are the kind of teachers Paul describes: They turn away from what is sound and wholesome and say what the people, with their itching ears, want to hear (2 Timothy 4:3). Jesus says that such prophets and teachers can be recognized by their fruit. Their fruit will not offer evidence of the age to come; it will be no different from that which you find in the world.

However, let us be clear. While we can identify false prophets, in view of all that Jesus teaches, we would be quite presumptuous to think we *know* who the "few" are and that we can give someone a printout of the citizens of the Kingdom. We would be even more presumptuous to say that "we" (whoever "we" are) are the few. But we are not presumptuous at all to say that the kingdom road is narrow, to assure others that only a few will find it, and to urge them (and ourselves) to make every effort to enter in, for indeed, the narrow road is the way to full life.

Questions for Study and Discussion

1. Share how you feel about this statement: "The other road begins with a narrow gate. It is not wide enough to accommodate all your stuff. There is much that will have to be left behind—mainly your 'self.' Humility and surrender are expected from the very beginning."

2. What experiences have you had or heard about that have shown you what it is like to put a lot into something only to have "destruction" be the result? How are you affected by what Jesus says about destruction?

3. The way is narrow and few find it, but a very high percentage of people around us think they are on the road to God. What thoughts, convictions, desires and decisions does that bring up in you?

24
Living the Sermon

L ooking back on what we have considered, would you
agree with us that the Sermon—this sermon on kingdom
living—is a masterpiece? There is nothing like it in all of spiritual literature. It fully addresses our humanity, and it calls
us to fully embrace God in his divinity. It shows us the life
that results when the divine and the human intersect and
overlap in the Kingdom.

We've learned from the get-go that it starts with being
humble, with being broken over our sins and being submissive to God. And you know how God is; he's given the two
of us ample opportunities to put all of this into practice day
after day. Maybe you too have been blessed with opportunities, even as you've been reading this book, to start putting
it into practice in new ways. We saw how important it is to
be reconciled to our brothers. We learned that we must love

our enemies, no matter how hard that may be. And maybe we're learning that it's sometimes harder to love your brother who offends you than an enemy on the other side of the world.

We saw that we should not store up possessions and that we should give to the needy. Opportunities to put that into practice abound.

We learned not to be anxious, and we learned how difficult it is. How are you doing with this?

Jesus told us not to have a judgmental attitude, and he's giving us plenty of chances to choose between being discerning and being critical.

So here we are at the end, and it comes down to these last words of Jesus:

> "Therefore everyone who hears these words of mine and puts them into practice is like a wise man who built his house on the rock. The rain came down, the streams rose, and the winds blew and beat against that house; yet it did not fall, because it had its foundation on the rock. But everyone who hears these words of mine and does not put them into practice is like a foolish man who built his house on sand. The rain came down, the streams rose, and the winds blew and beat against that house, and it fell with a great crash."
>
> When Jesus had finished saying these things, the crowds were amazed at his teaching, because he taught as one who had authority, and not as their teachers of the law. (Matthew 7:24–29)

This teaching about the Kingdom is exciting. Revolutionary. It calls us to become aliens from the future! All of it goes so much against the grain of our culture, of the American way of life (or the Mexican or the Iraqi or the Japanese).

Put It into Practice

It is absolutely worthless, however, if we don't live it. If we don't do what he said. If we don't put it into practice. Why bother? Why come to church and put on a masquerade if you're not going to do everything in your power to live this kingdom life?

Why read a book about the kingdom life? The grave danger for all of us is that we get excited about the ideas, and we fail to follow through…talk much but do little.

But wait. None of us is living it out perfectly. We all blow it. We all feel overwhelmed at times. This is not the point. Of all the billions and billions of people that lived on the earth only one man ever lived it perfectly. And he is the one who spoke these words. And he is full of grace toward those who are following him.

This brings us back to something else we learned: the power and importance of praying, of submitting ourselves to God's reign and rule, of seeking to do his will just like it is done in heaven. We can feel overwhelmed or discouraged or tempted to throw in the towel; this is when we need to ask, seek and knock, and keep on asking and seeking and knocking because our Heavenly Father wants to give us good gifts.

'We' Not 'Me'

And this reminds us of something else: This teaching is not about "me"; it is about "we." Remember the whole "corporate" concept? On our own, we are out of our depth. As we finished up this book, I (Steve) was driving across the state of Texas listening to '60s music, and the song "Help!" by the Beatles came on. The song tells of a man who once thought he could handle life on his own, but now has a more sober view and then cries out:

> Help me if you can, I'm feeling down
> And I do appreciate you being 'round.
> Help me get my feet back on the ground.
> Won't you please, please help me?

Appropriate, right? I need help. We all need help. And if we are aiming to follow Jesus on this Kingdom road, we are certainly going to need help. We have got to think "we" not "me."

Build on the Rock

Maybe we have sung the children's song about the wise man who built his house upon the rock one too many times. Maybe we think this story is kids' stuff. If so, we need to think again; Jesus is dead serious.

When our lives are not built on Jesus, we are not being obedient to his kingdom teaching, and we are building on sand, a great fall is coming. A disaster is waiting to happen.

When we are being open to his teachings, being faithful

in our marriages, resolving conflicts, loving our enemies, laying up our treasure in heaven, going and making disciples, and praying earnestly for his help in all of this, we are building on a rock. The wind and the storms will come, but our life will be built on the only true reality. Through it all, it will stand!

How do you build the kingdom life? You build it on Jesus. On the Rock.

Faith Is the Key

So where do we go from here? Well, where did the disciples go from there? It seems that as Matthew records the events, the next two chapters mention faith over and over. Not surprising is it? Faith.

A Roman centurion comes to Jesus with a servant who is paralyzed and suffering terribly. The man's attitude amazes Jesus, and he says to all those around them, "I have not found anyone in Israel with such great faith" (8:10).

Then a little later Jesus and his disciples are crossing the lake, and a storm comes up. The disciples are afraid they're going to die. Jesus says, "You of little faith, why are you so afraid?" (8:26).

In the next paragraph we see men bringing to Jesus a paralytic friend lying on a bed. The Bible says, "When Jesus saw their faith, he said to the paralytic, 'Take heart, son, your sins are forgiven'" (9:2). Later, in the face of unbelief and criticism, he heals the man to show that he had the authority to forgive sins.

A woman who had been suffering from an illness for twelve years comes up behind him and touches the fringe of his garment. Jesus says to her, "Take heart, daughter; your faith has healed you" (9:22).

Two blind men follow Jesus asking for him to have mercy on them. Jesus asks them, "Do you believe that I am able to do this?" They say, "Yes," so he tells them, "According to your faith be it done to you," and he healed them (9:28–29).

We are convinced that the key to living out the Sermon is our faith in God. Not faith in a plan. Not even faith in man. Not faith in our accomplishments. Faith in God—a creative and imaginative God. Just look at the universe around us, the incredible diversity of plants and animals, the amazing complexity of the human body, the awesome beauty that lies in outer space (things that we could not imagine until technology gave us the ability to see). Faith restores our creativity. We start believing in an Almighty God and we start waking up to what God is doing in our world and what he wants to do in us.

As Jesus saw so many people with so many needs, he told his disciples,

> "The harvest is plentiful but the workers are few.
> Ask the Lord of the harvest, therefore, to send out
> workers into his harvest field." (9:37–38)

In the next verses Matthew tells us that Jesus sent out his disciples to spread the message of the Kingdom throughout the land.

Knowing what we know about where the disciples were in their thinking and maturity at that point, we want to cry out, "Lord, what are you thinking?" The amazing thing is that Jesus knew them far better than they knew themselves, and he believed in them. He trusted them to get the job done with the help of his Spirit.

Yes, we have to have faith. The amazing thing to me is that God has faith in us. He has faith in you. God believes in you. Do you? God believes in his church and the people in it. Do you?

The Unshakeable Kingdom

There's only one Kingdom that the world has ever known that cannot be destroyed. Hebrews 12:28 says:

> Therefore, since we are receiving a kingdom that cannot be shaken, let us be thankful, and so worship God acceptably with reverence and awe.

Every empire the world has ever known has been shaken: e.g., Egyptian, Babylonian, Persian, Greek, Roman and British. The American Empire is being shaken. And someday it will fall. But we are citizens of the Kingdom of God, the Kingdom that cannot be shaken. It is built on the *Rock*.

The writer of Hebrews says we are receiving it. Are we? Are you? Are you praying, "Your Kingdom come, your will be done [in my life] on earth as it is in heaven"?

Questions for Study and Discussion

1. Why is it so important to listen carefully to how Jesus ends the Sermon? What distortions of his message does it help us avoid?
2. In this study what have you learned about the keys to putting his message into practice?
3. What decisions have you made as a result of this study?
4. In what ways is the practice of this kingdom life related to faith?
5. What role will the idea of "the unshakable Kingdom" play in helping you persevere even when you are greatly tested and challenged?

Epilogue
A Colony of Heaven

We have been to the mountain top. We have seen how life can be in the Kingdom of God as it breaks into the present age. We have seen a world where people are humble—where they learn from one another and open their lives up to whatever God wants. We have seen a world where people are committed—committed to showing mercy, making peace and enduring ugly opposition with grace and even joy. A world where ordinary people become extraordinarily distinctive and, like salt and light, have extraordinary impact.

We have seen a world where heart is more important than performance, where being technically right is not nearly as important as being inwardly right. A world where people want to resolve every conflict, forgive every wrong, love every enemy. A world where no one cares about getting the credit, where deeds done in secret bring even more satisfaction than deeds announced in the headlines.

We have seen a world where God rules—where his kingdom has come into the hearts of people and where doing his will is really all that matters. A world where people are not anxious because they are confident about the "much more of the Heavenly Father."

We have seen a world where people are interested not in judging one another self-righteously but in helping one another grow. A world where people find the greatest value in spiritual possessions, not in those things that will fade and perish. A world of builders whose foundations are solid and whose work endures through all that life throws at them.

The Impossible Dream?

It seems to me that there are fundamentally three responses one can have to all that Jesus says in this message.

1. "No way! Who could possibly do this?" Here is the person who looks at the Sermon on the Mount and says, "Give me a break. You don't really expect people to live like this do you? It's too hard. No one can do it. Trying will just make you feel guilty." This answer is heard not just from the man in the street, but from prominent psychologists who say Jesus had no right to place such heavy demands on people.

2. "It's wonderful. We should think more about it." I knew a man once who preached a sermon on this sermon of Jesus'. In it he spoke of "The Man from LaMancha" and the well-known song from that Broadway musical that talks of those who will "dream the impossible dream," and he preached in this sermon that this is exactly what Jesus was calling us to do—to go after the impossible. This man's sermon was masterfully constructed and delivered in dramatic fashion. After he preached it, there were those who wanted to hear it again, and eventually he was asked to come and deliver it in other churches. Then civic clubs invited him to share it, and colleges extended invitations. Just recently, I talked with him, and he told me he was still getting requests for it.

People like the nobility of the Sermon on the Mount. Its message touches something deep inside us. But while there are many who like to hear it played like some fine piece of chamber music, there are few who want to live it (see a similar problem in Ezekiel's day in Ezekiel 33:31–32). But Jesus said it would be this way: "…small is the gate and narrow the road that leads to life, and only a few find it." The world Jesus describes in this sermon will be found by only a few. Many will admire it from a distance, praise its grandeur and majesty; few will enter it.

3. "It's a great challenge, but it's God's will and I want it." Those with this spirit will become a world within the world—a colony of heaven on a troubled planet. The Kingdom of God will break into the present through them. They will become a world of faith in the midst of doubt—a world of hope in the midst of despair—a world of love in the midst of hate. "The few" who are in this new world will make more difference than all "the many" put together.

For years in the United States we have had big sweepstakes in which one person wins as much as $10 million spread over thirty years. I would presume there are such contests in other countries as well. Those who want to have an opportunity to win, dutifully send back as many as four replies. Many will enter. Only a very few will win. While one can send back his cards to make sure he is given a chance, the final outcome is out of any hopeful's hands. All one can do is wait for that phone call. For most it never comes.

Fortunately, this is not the way you find yourself in God's "few." Yes, *many* will miss it. Yes, only *a few* will find it. But it is entirely up to you and me. We can become part of those few in this brave new world. There's no lottery with God. We can commit ourselves to this sermon and the lordship of the one who spoke it. It's our choice. In one sense this sermon is "The Impossible Dream." No one can live it without error, but all those who put their hearts into it and go for it and go for it and go for it, will, by the grace of God, start changing their part of the world.

Make a Decision

Make a decision that you want in your life *every* attitude and *every* action described in this sermon. Do that today. Do it tomorrow. Do it forever. Don't sing the praises of this sermon. Put into practice its words. Get help. Get lots and lots of help. A person with the first three beatitudes in his or her heart wouldn't think of going it alone. Be totally committed to every principle, but be totally open about every struggle you have with obeying.

Finally, be confident. Be confident you can live these words in any circumstance. Of course, without the grace we have talked about from the very beginning of this volume, this would be impossible. But, be confident that *with God's help and his extraordinary grace that he lavishes on us,* you can do exactly what he planned for all of us to do when Jesus went up on a mountainside, sat down and taught us "Seek first the kingdom of God...."

(This epilogue by Tom A. Jones first appeared in the book *First...the Kingdom* published seventeen years ago. With just a few additions, it seemed an appropriate way to end this book.)

NOTES

Introduction

1. Augustine, writing in the fifth century, seems to be the first person to refer to this message as the "Sermon on the Mount."

2. I (Tom) acknowledge here the influence of D.M. Lloyd-Jones' book *The Sermon on the Mount*. I read this book years ago and found his introduction particularly helpful. Those familiar with his work will certainly see that some of what we are calling "rules for the road" were suggested by him. Also note that later Steve and I will take issue with some of his conclusions.

3. Philip Yancey, *The Jesus I Never Knew* (Grand Rapids: Zondervan, 1995), 130.

4. Glen Stassen and David Gushee, *Kingdom Ethics* (Downer's Grove, IL: IVP, 2007), 35.

5. Stassen and Gushee, 10.

6. Stassen and Gushee, 11.

7. John Howard Yoder, *The Politics of Jesus* (Grand Rapids: Wm. B. Eerdmans, 1972), 61.

Chapter 3
Those Who Mourn

1. John Stott, *Christian Counter Culture: The Message of the Sermon on the Mount* (Downer's Grove, IL: IVP, 1978), 41.

Chapter 5
Hunger and Thirst

1. *The Leaders Resource Handbook* (Spring Hill, TN: DPI, 1998), 143–147.

2. Stassen and Gushee, 42–43, 53.

3. R.C.H. Lenski, *The Interpretation of St. Matthew's Gospel* (Minneapolis: Augsburg Publishing House, 1961), 189.

4. William Barclay, *The Gospel According to Matthew* (Philadelphia: The Westminster Press, 1958), 96.

Chapter 6
The Merciful

1. Alvin J. Schmidt, *How Christianity Changed the World* (Grand Rapids: Zondervan, 2004), 125–170.

Chapter 7
The Pure in Heart

1. D.M. Lloyd-Jones, *The Sermon on the Mount* (Grand Rapids: Wm. B. Eerdmans, 1959), 109.

Chapter 11
Kingdom Righteousness

1. According to William D. Mounce, author of *Basics of Biblical Greek* (Grand Rapids: Zondervan, 2009) pages 288 and 296: "the double negative with the subjunctive is an emphatic negative in the future. It is used 85 times in the New Testament."

Chapter 12
Kingdom Relationships

1. Thomas Jones and Steve Brown, *One Another: Transformational Relationships in the Body of Christ* (Spring Hill, TN: DPI, 2008).

Chapter 14
Kingdom Marriage

1. David P. Scaer, *The Sermon on the Mount* (St. Louis: Concordia Publishing, 2000), 119.

2. Scaer, 172–177.

Chapter 17
Kingdom Love for Enemies

1. Dietrich Bonhoeffer, *The Cost of Discipleship* (New York: Simon and Shuster, 1937, 1959, 1975), 146.

2. Bonhoeffer, 146–147.

3. Bonhoeffer, 148.

4. Bonhoeffer, 152.

5. Bonhoeffer, 148.

6. John Howard Yoder, "Living the Disarmed Life," *A Matter of Faith, Sojourners' Magazine Study Guide*, (January 1982).

Chapter 18
Kingdom Rewards

1. Barclay, 185.
2. Barclay, 239–240.

Chapter 19
The Kingdom Prayer

1. Scaer, 172–177.

Chapter 20
Kingdom Treasure

1. Venard Eller, *The Simple Life* (available free on the Internet).

Chapter 21
Kingdom Judgments

1. R.V.G. Tasker, *The Gospel According to St. Matthew* (Grand Rapids: Wm. B. Eerdmans Publishing Company, 1973), 79.

SELECTED BIBLIOGRAPHY

Barclay, William. *The Gospel of Matthew*. Philadelphia: The Westminster Press, 1958.

Bonhoeffer, Dietrich. *The Cost of Discipleship*. New York: Simon and Shuster, 1937, 1959, 1975.

Carsaon, D.A. *Jesus' Sermon on the Mount and His Confrontation with the World*. Grand Rapids: Baker Books, 1987.

Eller, Vernard. *The Simple Life*. Grand Rapids: Wm. B. Eerdmans, 1973.

Lenski, R.C.H. *The Interpretation of St. Matthew's Gospel*. Minneapolis: Augsburg Publishing House, 1961.

Lloyd-Jones, D.M. *The Sermon on the Mount*. Grand Rapids: Wm. B. Eerdmans, 1959.

Scaer, David P. *The Sermon on the Mount*. St. Louis: Concordia Publishing, 2000.

Schaefer, Steve. *Living in the Overlap*. Enumclaw, WA: Winepress Publishing, 2010.

Schmidt, Alvin J. *How Christianity Changed the World*. Grand Rapids: Zondervan, 2004.

Stassen, Glen H. and David P. Gushee. *Kingdom Ethics*. Downers Grove, IL: IVP Academic, 2007.

Stott, John. *Christian Counter Culture: The Message of the Sermon on the Mount*. Downer's Grove, IL: IVP, 1978.

Tasker, R.V.G. *The Gospel According to St. Matthew*. Grand Rapids: Wm. B. Eerdmans Publishing Company, 1973.

Yoder, John Howard. *The Politics of Jesus*. Grand Rapids: Wm. B. Eerdmans, 1972.

Young, Brad H. *Jesus: The Jewish Theologian*. Peabody, MA: Hendrickson Publishers, 1995.